KITCHEN CHEMISTRY

Cool Crystals, Rockin' Reactions, and Magical Mixtures

with Hands-On Science Activities

☑ BAKING SO
☑ ½ C VINE
☐ Hot wa
☑ SPOON

Cynthia Light Brown
Illustrated by Micah Rauch

Titles in the **Build It Yourself Accessible Science** Set

 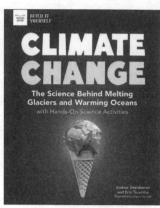 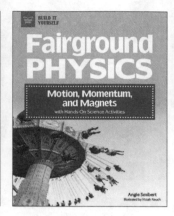 

Check out more titles at www.nomadpress.net

Nomad Press

A division of Nomad Communications

10 9 8 7 6 5 4 3 2 1

This book was manufactured by Versa Press, East Peoria, Illinois
March 2020, Job #J19-12317
ISBN Softcover: 978-1-61930-887-9
ISBN Hardcover: 978-1-61930-884-8

Educational Consultant, Marla Conn

Questions regarding the ordering of this book should be addressed to
Nomad Press
2456 Christian St., White River Junction, VT 05001
www.nomadpress.net

Printed in the United States.

CONTENTS

Interested in Primary Sources? Look for this icon.

Use a smartphone or tablet app to scan the QR code and explore more! Photos are also primary sources because a photograph takes a picture at the moment something happens. You can find a list of URLs on the Resources page. If the QR code doesn't work, try searching the internet with the Keyword Prompts to find other helpful sources.

🔎 kitchen chemistry

PERIODIC TABLE OF ELEMENTS

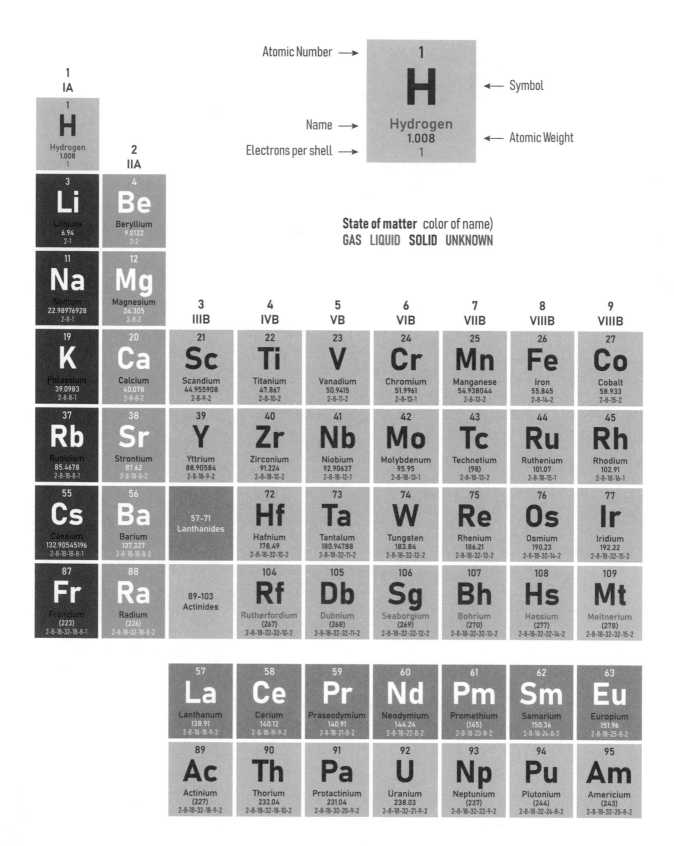

PERIODIC TABLE OF ELEMENTS

Subcategory in the metal-metalloid-nonmetal trend (color of background)

- ◼ Alkali metals
- ◼ Alkaline earth metals
- ◼ Transition metals
- ◼ Lanthanides
- ◼ Actinides
- ◼ Post-transition metals
- ◼ Metalloids
- ◼ Reactive nonmetals
- ◼ Noble gases
- ◼ Unknown chemical properties

			13 IIIA	14 IVA	15 VA	16 VIA	17 VIIA	18 VIIIA
								2 **He** Helium 4.0026 2
			5 **B** Boron 10.81 2-3	6 **C** Carbon 12.011 2-4	7 **N** Nitrogen 14.007 2-5	8 **O** Oxygen 15.999 2-6	9 **F** Fluorine 18.998 2-7	10 **Ne** Neon 20.180 2-8
10 VIIIB	11 IB	12 IIB	13 **Al** Aluminium 26.982 2-8-3	14 **Si** Silicon 28.085 2-8-4	15 **P** Phosphorus 30.974 2-8-5	16 **S** Sulfur 32.06 2-8-6	17 **Cl** Chlorine 35.45 2-8-7	18 **Ar** Argon 39.948 2-8-8
28 **Ni** Nickel 58.693 2-8-16-2	29 **Cu** Copper 63.546 2-8-18-1	30 **Zn** Zinc 65.38 2-8-18-2	31 **Ga** Gallium 69.723 2-8-18-3	32 **Ge** Germanium 72.630 2-8-18-4	33 **As** Arsenic 74.922 2-8-18-5	34 **Se** Selenium 78.971 2-8-18-6	35 **Br** Bromine 79.904 2-8-18-7	36 **Kr** Krypton 83.798 2-8-18-8
46 **Pd** Palladium 106.42 2-8-18-18	47 **Ag** Silver 107.87 2-8-18-18-1	48 **Cd** Cadmium 112.41 2-8-18-18-2	49 **In** Indium 114.82 2-8-18-18-3	50 **Sn** Tin 118.71 2-8-18-18-4	51 **Sb** Antimony 121.76 2-8-18-18-5	52 **Te** Tellurium 127.60 2-8-18-18-6	53 **I** Iodine 126.90 2-8-18-18-7	54 **Xe** Xenon 131.29 2-8-18-18-8
78 **Pt** Platinum 195.08 2-8-18-32-17-1	79 **Au** Gold 196.97 2-8-18-32-18-1	80 **Hg** Mercury 200.59 2-8-18-32-18-2	81 **Tl** Thallium 204.38 2-8-18-32-18-3	82 **Pb** Lead 207.2 2-8-18-32-18-4	83 **Bi** Bismuth 208.98 2-8-18-32-18-5	84 **Po** Polonium (209) 2-8-18-32-18-6	85 **At** Astatine (210) 2-8-18-32-18-7	86 **Rn** Radon (222) 2-8-18-32-18-8
110 **Ds** Darmstadtium (281) 2-8-18-32-32-17-1	111 **Rg** Roentgenium (282) 2-8-18-32-32-17-2	112 **Cn** Copernicium (285) 2-8-18-32-32-18-2	113 **Nh** Nihonium (286) 2-8-18-32-32-18-3	114 **Fl** Flerovium (289) 2-8-18-32-32-18-4	115 **Mc** Moscovium (290) 2-8-18-32-32-18-5	116 **Lv** Livermorium (293) 2-8-18-32-32-18-6	117 **Ts** Tennessine (294) 2-8-18-32-32-18-7	118 **Og** Oganesson (294) 2-8-18-32-32-18-8

64 **Gd** Gadolinium 157.25 2-8-18-25-9-2	65 **Tb** Terbium 158.93 2-8-18-27-8-2	66 **Dy** Dysprosium 162.50 2-8-18-28-8-2	67 **Ho** Holmiun 164.93 2-8-18-29-8-2	68 **Er** Erbium 167.26 2-8-18-30-8-2	69 **Tm** Thulium 168.93 2-8-18-31-8-2	70 **Yb** Ytterbium 173.05 2-8-18-32-8-2	71 **Lu** Lutetium 174.97 2-8-18-32-9-2
96 **Cm** Curium (247) 2-8-18-32-25-9-2	97 **Bk** Berkelium (247) 2-8-18-32-27-8-2	98 **Cf** Californium (251) 2-8-18-32-28-8-2	99 **Es** Einsteinium (252) 2-8-18-32-29-8-2	100 **Fm** Fermium (257) 2-8-18-32-30-8-2	101 **Md** Mendelevium (258) 2-8-18-32-31-8-2	102 **No** Nobelium (259) 2-8-18-32-32-8-2	103 **Lr** Lawrencium (266) 2-8-18-32-32-8-3

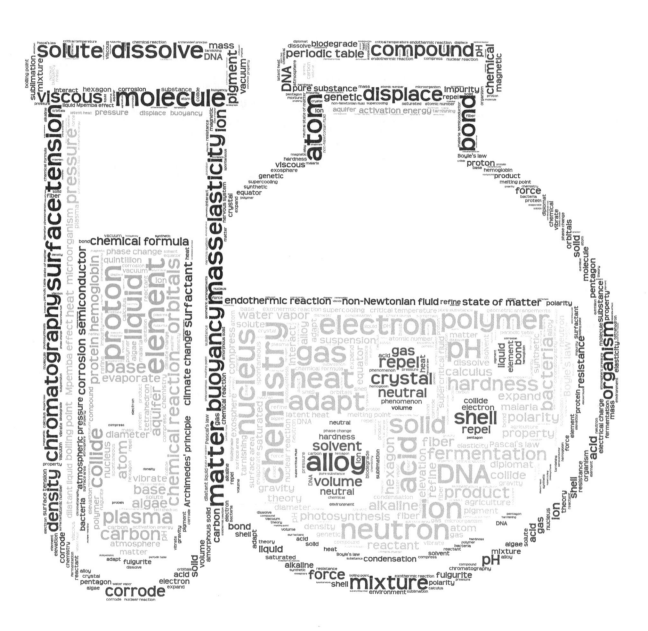

CHEMISTRY
MATTERS!

What makes something soft or hard? What makes something a solid, liquid, or gas? Why does water change from solid ice to liquid water to water vapor? Chemistry can tell you! Chemistry is at the heart of how everything works—it's the science of change.

You might think that chemists are people who work in labs and wear white coats. But that's not necessarily true! Chemistry is everywhere and chemistry can be studied everywhere—including in your kitchen, classroom, and backyard. And anyone can explore chemistry with fun experiments and activities. The rule is to keep it safe.

ESSENTIAL QUESTION

What is chemistry?

WORDS TO KNOW

water vapor: the gas state of water.

chemistry: the study of the properties of substances and how they react with one another.

1

WORDS TO KNOW

matter: anything that has weight and takes up space. Almost everything is made of matter!

atom: the smallest particle of matter that cannot be broken down by chemical means. An atom is made up of a nucleus of protons and neutrons surrounded by a cloud of electrons.

molecule: a group of atoms bound together to form matter.

solid: one of the three states of matter. The particles in a solid are bound together tightly. A solid has a definite shape and volume and does not flow.

liquid: one of the three states of matter. The particles in a liquid cluster together and flow. A liquid has a definite volume, but takes the shape of its container.

gas: one of the three states of matter. The particles in a gas are not bound to each other and move very fast in all directions. A gas does not have a definite shape or volume.

interact: how things act when they are together.

Chemistry is the study of **matter** and how it changes. Matter is anything that has mass and takes up space. That means everything on Earth, in the solar system, and in the galaxy is made of matter. Including you! What about the book or tablet you are holding? What about your dog? What about the water you're drinking? What about the air you're breathing?

MATTER—
it's all matter!

Matter is made up of **atoms** and **molecules**, known as the basic building blocks of matter. Think of a bucket full of water. This bucket contains more molecules of water than there are buckets of water in the entire Atlantic Ocean! Atoms are pretty small.

States of Matter

There are three common states of matter: **solid**, **liquid**, and **gas**. With enough heat or cooling, a substance can change from one to another. A good example is liquid water, which when heated can change into water vapor, or if cooled can change into ice. Ice can melt back into water and water vapor can cool to change back into liquid water. When you see water droplets form on the outside of your cold glass of lemonade on a hot summer day, that's an example of water vapor changing into liquid water.

These atoms and molecules **interact** in different ways. The interactions decide what kind of matter those atoms and molecules will be. And, of course, that can change—remember, chemistry is the science of how things change. We'll learn more about atoms and molecules in Chapter 1.

THE MIND OF A SCIENTIST

Scientists have a special way of looking at the world, and you can, too. Here's what you do. Notice things. Pay attention. Look around. Be curious. That's it. That's the secret to being a scientist.

If Benjamin Franklin (1706–1790) hadn't noticed how the water changed behind ships as they sailed, he wouldn't have experimented with oil and water (see Chapter 5 to learn more). If you notice what's going on around you, you'll see all kinds of things to explore.

Water as a solid, liquid, and gas
credit: Ajith Kumar (CC BY 2.0)

KITCHEN CHEMISTRY

WORDS TO KNOW

expand: to spread out and take up more space.

substance: the physical material from which something is made.

volume: the amount of space inside an object.

carbon: a kind of atom that is the building block of most living things, as well as diamonds, charcoal, and graphite.

Water **EXPANDS** as it freezes, which is different from most other **substances**. An ice cube takes up about 9 percent **MORE VOLUME** than the water used to make it.

If you see something you don't understand or that doesn't make sense, find out more about it. That may involve some research in a library, but it might also involve trying an experiment, which is another important—and even more fun—way to investigate. Ask questions such as "Why?" and "What would happen if . . .?"

After you try an experiment or a project in this book, you can also change the experiment a bit to see what happens. Note that if you want to use new materials, though, check with an adult first to make sure the experiment will be safe.

Here's the important thing about making changes in a project: Only make one change at a time. Otherwise, you won't know which of your changes made a difference in the results.

Boiling water freezing almost instantly

credit: Alfredo Ristol (CC BY 2.0)

Believe what you see, not what you think you should see. If Erasto Mpemba (1950–) hadn't believed his own eyes, he never would have figured out that boiling water can freeze faster than warm water (read about him in Chapter 7). When you try an experiment or make a change to one you've already done, try to predict what might happen next.

Even if your results aren't what you expected, you can learn something. If something doesn't work the way you thought it would, maybe you made a mistake. For example, you might have put in too much of one ingredient. But maybe your results show you something new. Scientists make new discoveries all the time based on "mistakes."

Share and compare. Scientists often work together to solve problems. If Harry Kroto (1939–2016), Richard Smalley (1943–2005), and Robert Curl (1933–) hadn't worked together as a team, they probably would not have discovered the buckyball or won the Nobel Prize. You'll read about them in Chapter 1.

Watch a video about the buckyball! We'll learn more about carbon later in the book. Is it surprising to you that major scientific discoveries are still being made? In fact, there are incredible breakthroughs in science every day. Maybe you'll be the next person to make one!

🔎 Scishow buckyball

WORDS TO KNOW

environment: everything in nature, living and nonliving, including animals, plants, rocks, soil, and water.

agriculture: growing plants and raising animals for food and other products.

Keep track of your results and share them with others. Maybe together you can figure out why your project or experiment turned out as it did.

Today, scientists are using chemistry to improve our daily lives. Through chemistry, we can make products such as food, clothing, and construction materials even better. Chemists are also working to protect the **environment**, improve **agriculture**, and find new sources of energy. It's an exciting time to be a chemist!

Good Science Practices

Every good scientist keeps a science journal! Scientists use the scientific method to keep their experiments organized. Choose a notebook to use as your science journal. As you read through this book and do the activities, keep track of your observations and record each step in a scientific method worksheet, like the one shown here.

Question: What are we trying to find out? What problem are we trying to solve?

Research: What information is already known?

Hypothesis/Prediction: What do I think the answer will be?

Equipment: What supplies do I need?

Method: What steps will I follow?

Results: What happened? Why?

Each chapter of this book begins with a question to help guide your exploration of chemistry. Keep the question in your mind as you read the chapter. At the end of each chapter, use your science journal to record your thoughts and answers. Does your answer change as you read the chapter?

ESSENTIAL QUESTION

What is chemistry?

HOW CHEMICALS
CHANGE

Humans use **chemicals** every day. That's because everything is made of chemicals—including us! You'll read later about how chemicals react and form new ones and how their **properties** can change. For now, let's work on noticing different substances that change.

❯ **Make a list in your science journal of different substances** that you see changing. Maybe it's a liquid that changes into a solid or gas, or vice versa. Maybe you see something change color, shape, texture, or temperature. Here are some ideas to help you think of places or types of items where you might find substances that change.

* Food or other items in your kitchen

* Your fireplace

* Your backyard

* A nearby pond or woods

* A houseplant

❯ **Check on your substances every day for a week or two.** Make drawings or take notes in your science journal. How do they change? Do they grow bigger or smaller? Do they rot or grow? Do they get smelly? Do they change color?

❯ **As you read through this book, go back to your list and try to identify** whether the changes you saw were from a **chemical reaction** or because of changes in the surroundings, such as changing temperature. Were there any surprises?

Think About It

Everything around you, and in you, is in a constant state of change. Change might be helpful or hurtful, but it's going to happen no matter what.

WORDS TO KNOW

chemical: the pure form of a substance. Some chemicals can be combined or broken up to create new chemicals.

property: a quality or feature of something. The way something is.

chemical reaction: the rearrangement of atoms in a substance to make a new chemical substance.

Chapter 1

THE SMALL STUFF:
ATOMS &
MOLECULES

A star. The air. A bee. Clouds. Hot lava. Bicycles. Icebergs. You. All these things have different shapes, colors, temperatures, textures, and densities. In other ways, though, they're all the same. They are all made of matter and they are all made up of relatively few kinds of particles.

It's the arrangement of those particles that makes all the difference in the world. It even makes all the difference in the universe. How those particles are arranged means the difference between a human, an insect, a raindrop, and fog. Let's take a closer look at these particles.

ESSENTIAL QUESTION

What makes one substance different from another?

ATOMS EVERYWHERE

Atoms are the basic building blocks of everything. They are so tiny that you can't see them, even with most microscopes. Every atom is composed of **protons**, **neutrons**, and **electrons**.

The protons have a positive **electrical charge**. They are balanced by electrons, which have a negative charge, and neutrons, which don't have a charge at all—they are neutral. The protons and neutrons clump together in the **nucleus**, or center, of the atom, and the electrons spin around the nucleus.

Scientists used to think that electrons travel around the nucleus in definite circular patterns. Now, we know that electrons don't follow a perfect circle around the nucleus but are more likely to be found in certain areas, called **orbitals**. If you could take a picture of all the places that electrons go, it would look a bit like a swarm of bees (electrons) around a beehive (the nucleus). You wouldn't be able to predict where an individual bee would go, but you'd know it would stay close to the beehive.

Most of an atom is empty space though. If the outer orbit of an electron for hydrogen were two miles wide, which is the size of a small city, then the proton in the nucleus would be the size of a golf ball. Everything else is empty space.

Although we can't see an atom with our eyes—it's too small—David Nadlinger took a photo of light emitted by a single atom. **Check it out here!**

🔍 National Post strontium atom

DENSITY is a property of matter. It is how tightly packed or spread apart **MOLECULES** are in matter.

The nucleus is held together very tightly—so tightly that it takes a **nuclear reaction** to split one. But the electrons aren't held as tightly, so it's easier to add an electron to an atom or take away an electron from an atom. And those electrons don't always like to stay in one place. They often move around from one nucleus to another. It is this movement of electrons that allows atoms to bond together to make all the different substances in and around you. And that's what chemistry is all about.

ELEMENTS

We call a substance that is made up of just one type of atom an **element**. Pure gold is an element because it contains only gold atoms. Oxygen is an element because it only has oxygen atoms. Ninety-four different kinds of atoms, or elements, occur naturally. Scientists have managed to create another 24 elements in science labs. All matter, from the smallest speck to the largest star, is made of these elements.

What makes the elements different from each other? It's the number of protons in the nucleus of an atom, called the **atomic number**. A hydrogen atom always has one proton. An oxygen atom always has eight protons. And a gold atom always has 79 protons.

Is there a water atom? No! Most things aren't pure elements—instead, they are made of molecules. Molecules are simply two or more atoms bonded together. The atoms can be the same kind of atom, but more often are different types. A water molecule is made up of two hydrogen atoms and one oxygen atom.

The number of
MOLECULES
you breathe in with
only one breath
of air is more
than the number of
GRAINS OF SAND
on the entire earth.

The **bond** that holds molecules together isn't a fixed thing, like a stick or string, even though we draw it that way sometimes. A bond is a **force**. Atoms can still wiggle, or **vibrate**, when they're bonded.

Different kinds of bonds are possible, but all bonds have atoms sharing or trading their electrons. Molecules can be as simple as two atoms bonded together. They can also be very complex, with thousands or even millions of atoms bonded together. These bonds make it possible for us to have millions of different kinds of natural substances, not just 94.

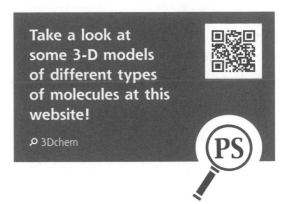

Take a look at some 3-D models of different types of molecules at this website!

🔎 3Dchem

PS

The element gold and its symbol, AU, showing 79 electrons circling the nucleus
credit: James St. John (CC BY 2.0)

ion: an atom that has an unequal number of protons and electrons. An ion has a positive charge if it has lost an electron and it has a negative charge if it has gained an electron.

chemical formula: a representation of a substance or of a chemical reaction using symbols for its elements.

IONS

Each atom has an equal number of electrons and protons, so the negative charge of the electrons and the positive charge of the protons balance each other out. As a result, atoms have a neutral charge. For example, gold has 79 protons and 79 electrons. Neon has 10 protons and 10 electrons.

Some elements tend to gain or lose one or more electrons, but the element still stays the same. Hydrogen is one of the elements that tends to lose its electron. It's still hydrogen, but without its electron it has a positive charge. When an atom has lost or gained an electron and has a positive or negative charge, we call it an **ion**.

Vintage Phones

How would you like to use a cell phone that keeps a charge for only 35 minutes, weighs 2 pounds (that's about six times as heavy as cell phones today), and is the size of a large brick? That was the first cell phone, in 1973. Its nickname was "The Brick!" Cell phones have undergone all kinds of developments since 1973, but without the humble lithium ion, they couldn't be as small and light as they are now. Lithium is an element with three protons and three electrons. It can lose an electron to become a positive ion. That lithium ion (with a symbol of Li+) is the basis for lightweight, rechargeable batteries that hold their charge for hours. In lithium-ion batteries, the lithium ions travel from the positive to the negative end of a battery as you charge the battery, then in the opposite direction as you use the battery. Scientists are working on ways to extend the life of those batteries even more for computers, cell phones, and even cars by using lithium ions or other materials.

CHEMICAL FORMULAS

If you had to write a math equation, you probably wouldn't write, "Twenty-eight plus fourteen equals forty-two." It would take too long to write and it would be hard to read quickly. You would write, "28 + 14 = 42." Chemistry is the same way. Chemists write chemical equations all the time, and it would take too long if they had to spell everything out. So, chemists use symbols in **chemical formulas**, just as we do in math.

A CHEMICAL FORMULA is the way we PRESENT INFORMATION about the contents of a molecule.

The symbol for each element is a letter or pair of letters. The chemical formula lists all the elements that form each molecule and uses a small number to the bottom right of an element's symbol to stand for the number of atoms of that element. For example, the chemical formula for water is H_2O. That tells us that a water molecule is made up of two hydrogen ("H" and "2") atoms and one oxygen ("O") atom. Carbon dioxide is CO_2, meaning it has one carbon ("C") atom and two oxygen ("O" and "2") atoms.

The **periodic table** logically organizes all the known elements. Russian chemist Dmitri Mendeleev (1834–1907) came up with the periodic table of elements in 1869. He was even able to anticipate where on the chart new elements would go before they were actually discovered! He left gaps where the known elements didn't seem to fit according to their properties. Compare Mendeleev's periodic table with the modern periodic table on pages iv and v.

The periodic table is an ingredients list for a recipe to make everything in the universe! It arranges the elements in a way that shows many of their properties and relationships to each other. The horizontal rows are called periods and the vertical columns are called groups. The groups, numbered 1 through 18 (on the page iv version), are listed at the top of each column. Some tables still include the Roman numerals I through VIII for the groups, as shown below—these were used for most of the twentieth century until they were replaced in 1990 by the numbers we use today.

Series	Zero Group	Group I	Group II	Group III	Group IV	Group V	Group VI	Group VII	Group VIII			
0	x											
1	y	Hydrogen H=1·008											
2	Helium He=4·0	Lithium Li=7·03	Beryllium Be=9·1	Boron B=11·0	Carbon C=12·0	Nitrogen N=14·04	Oxygen O=16·00	Fluorine F=19·0				
3	Neon Ne=19·9	Sodium Na=23·05	Magnesium Mg=24·1	Aluminium Al=27·0	Silicon Si=28·4	Phosphorus P=31·0	Sulphur S=32·06	Chlorine Cl=35·45				
4	Argon Ar=38	Potassium K=39·1	Calcium Ca=40·1	Scandium Sc=44·1	Titanium Ti=48·1	Vanadium V=51·4	Chromium Cr=52·1	Manganese Mn=55·0	Iron Fe=55·9	Cobalt Co=59	Nickel Ni=59	(Cu)
5		Copper Cu=63·6	Zinc Zn=65·4	Gallium Ga=70·0	Germanium Ge=72·3	Arsenic As=75·0	Selenium Se=79	Bromine Br=79·95				
6	Krypton Kr=81·8	Rubidium Rb=85·4	Strontium Sr=87·6	Yttrium Y=89·0	Zirconium Zr=90·6	Niobium Nb=94·0	Molybdenum Mo=96·0	—	Ruthenium Ru=101·7	Rhodium Rh=103·0	Palladium Pd=106·5	(Ag)
7		Silver Ag=107·9	Cadmium Cd=112·4	Indium In=114·0	Tin Sn=119·0	Antimony Sb=120·0	Tellurium Te=127	Iodine I=127				
8	Xenon Xe=128	Osmium Os=133·9	Barium Ba=137·4	Lanthanum La=139	Cerium Ce=140	—	—		—	—	—	(—)
9		—	—		—	—	—	—				
10	—	—	—	Ytterbium Yb=173	—	Tantalum Ta=183	Tungsten W=184	—	Osmium Os=191	Iridium Ir=193	Platinum Pt=194·9	(Au)
11		Gold Au=197·2	Mercury Hg=200·0	Thallium Tl=204·1	Lead Pb=206·9	Bismuth Bi=208		—	—				
12	—	—	Radium Rd=224	—	Thorium Th=232	—	Uranium U=239					

This is Mendeleev's periodic table from 1904. Compare it to the one on pages iv and v. What is different about them? What is similar?

How Small is a Molecule?

Molecules and atoms are so tiny that it's hard to even imagine them. A single grain of sugar contains about 1,000,000,000,000,000,000—or a **quintillion**—molecules. How big is a quintillion? If each molecule was the size of a penny, then a grain of sugar would be as wide and long as a football field, with its pennies stacked almost 100,000 miles high. That would be almost halfway to the moon. Think about the size of the cavity that you'd get from that much sugar!

For each element, the table shows the atomic number, its name, and its symbol—which is used in chemical equations. The symbol is often the first letter or two of the element's name, such as C for carbon or O for oxygen, but sometimes it comes from a Latin name, such as Fe for iron, from the Latin word *ferrum* for iron.

As they discover **NEW ELEMENTS,** scientists continue to add them to the **PERIODIC TABLE.** In 2016, four new elements were added: Nihonium (Nh), **Moscovium (Mc), Tennessine (Ts), and Oganesson (Og).**

CARBON

Diamonds, when cut, are sparkly and beautiful. They are also the hardest substance known. Graphite, which is used in pencils, is dull and gray and so soft you can write with it. About as different as you can get, right?

Wrong. Diamonds and graphite are very much alike. They are both made of exactly the same element—carbon. And nothing else. In fact, in the laboratory, scientists can turn graphite into diamonds using high **pressure**.

WORDS TO KNOW

tetrahedron: a shape with four triangular faces.

hexagon: a six-sided shape.

pentagon: a five-sided shape.

hemoglobin: a substance in red blood cells that combines with and carries oxygen around the body. Hemoglobin gives blood its red color.

polymer: a long-chained molecule made up of smaller molecules, called monomers, linked together.

genetic: traits that are passed from parent to child.

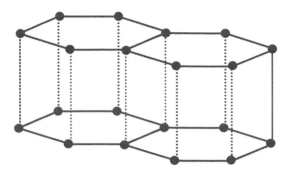

Graphite atom structure

The reason diamonds and graphite have such different qualities is not because of what they're made of but because of how the carbon is put together. If you could shrink to the size of an atom and walk around inside a diamond and a piece of graphite, they would look quite different. Each carbon atom in a diamond is joined to four others to make a **tetrahedron**, and all the bonds are strong. Triangles make very strong shapes.

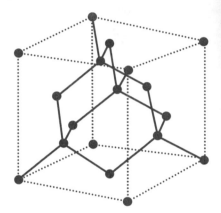

Diamond atom structure

Buckyballs!

Another form of carbon was discovered by a group of scientists in 1985. Harry Kroto, Richard Smalley, and Robert Curl called their discovery buckminsterfullerene, or "buckyball." It was named after architect Richard Buckminster Fuller (1895–1983) for the dome-shaped buildings he designed. In a buckyball, 60 atoms are bonded in patterns of **hexagons** and **pentagons** to make a shape like a soccer ball. Other similar carbon structures have 28, 70, or even more atoms. Buckytubes, or nanotubes, are hollow, tube-shaped structures also made completely from carbon.

Giant Molecule!

Just how complicated can carbon-based molecules be? Take a look at **hemoglobin**, which is what makes blood red. Hemoglobin is the part of blood that carries oxygen from our lungs to the rest of our body—without it, we couldn't live. The chemical formula for hemoglobin is $C_{2954}H_{516}N_{780}O_{806}S_{12}Fe_4$. That's 2,954 atoms of carbon (C), 516 atoms of hydrogen (H), 780 atoms of nitrogen (N), 806 atoms of oxygen (O), 12 atoms of sulfur (S), and 4 atoms of iron. All of that is in each hemoglobin molecule, and all those atoms are arranged in a very specific way. That's one complex molecule!

In graphite, the carbon atoms bond in rings of six, or hexagons, which form sheets of carbon. The sheets look like a honeycomb and are very strong—as strong as diamonds—but the bonds between the sheets are very weak and break easily. When the weak bonds break, the sheets slide against each other and separate. When you write with your pencil, some of the graphite is breaking off to make a mark. As you write, you leave a trail of carbon behind on the paper.

CARBON can form POLYMERS, which are huge, complicated molecules of almost ENDLESS CHAINS.

POLYMERS

Carbon is the most important atom in living creatures. Without it, life—at least, life as we know it—could not exist. For life to exist, large, complex molecules, called **polymers**, are needed to store energy, pass on **genetic** information, and form tissue. No matter how it's put together, carbon is a strange and wonderful substance.

KITCHEN CHEMISTRY

WORDS TO KNOW

synthetic: something made of artificial materials, using a chemical reaction.

deoxyribonucleic acid (DNA): the molecule in all living things that carries genetic information.

protein: a group of large molecules. Proteins are an essential part of all living things.

fiber: a thin thread.

Not everything can form polymers. Water, for example, can't link to itself in long chains. Carbon has many special characteristics, such as the ability to form more than one bond per atom. As a result, carbon can form long chains of polymers—like a very long chain of paper clips. Some polymers are natural, such as your hair. Many others, including plastic milk cartons, are **synthetic**, or manufactured.

If it weren't for polymers, you wouldn't be you! Who you are is determined in part by **deoxyribonucleic acid (DNA)**, better known as DNA. These are the big molecules in your body that contain coding for all sorts of things, from the color of your hair to whether you are left-handed or right-handed. DNA, along with all **proteins**, is a polymer.

Now that you have a good grasp of the building blocks of chemistry, let's shake things up a bit. Let's look at what happens when you mix substances together!

ESSENTIAL QUESTION

What makes one substance different from another?

Great Inventions

Kevlar is a polymer. It's a special kind of **fiber** used to make body armor and sports equipment that is five times stronger than steel. Kevlar was first created in 1965 by Stephanie Kwolek (1923–2014). When Kwolek was a young girl, she thought she might want to be a fashion designer. But her love of science led her to chemistry. She worked at a company called DuPont, researching high-performance fibers. In a way, she still ended up designing clothing, because one of the most important uses of Kevlar is in bulletproof vests. Bulletproof vests are even worn by police dogs. And Kwolek's invention opened up the whole new field of polymer chemistry. About her work as a chemist, Kwolek said, "You have to be prepared in chemistry. You have to have a certain background. You have to be inquisitive about things. You have to have an open mind."

POP A BALLOON
WITH NO HANDS!

Try this "trick" where you pop a balloon without touching it.

➤ **Blow up one of the water balloons and tie it off.** Gently rub a few drops of water on the balloon. Does anything happen? Record what happens in your journal.

➤ **Peel an orange.** Do you smell anything while you're peeling?

➤ **Hold the shiny part of the orange peel** toward the balloon, and twist the peel to squeeze some of the juices onto the balloon. Record what happens to it in your journal.

When you SMELL something, molecules from the substance travel through the air and land inside your nostrils. When you smell oranges, you're breathing in LIMONENE MOLECULES!

WHAT'S HAPPENING?

The juice from the orange peel dissolved the balloon just enough for the air pressure in the balloon to make the balloon . . . pop!

Why does orange peel juice dissolve the balloon when water doesn't? Water balloons are made of rubber, which is a polymer made of hydrogen and carbon. Orange peel juice has a chemical in it called limonene. Like rubber, limonene molecules are made of hydrogen and carbon atoms, but arranged differently. Chemists have a saying that "like dissolves like." That means that a chemical can more easily dissolve another substance when they're similar. Limonene is similar to rubber, but water isn't.

Think About It

Try using other foods from your kitchen, such as cooking oil, dish soap, vinegar, or lemon or lime peels. Record what happens. Which substances do you think have chemicals in them that are similar to rubber?

MAKE
MERINGUES

Meringue is that white, fluffy-looking stuff you see on the tops of some pies, such as lemon meringue pie—yum! Meringue is not only delicious, but it's also a fascinating polymer. This recipe for meringue cookies works best if you make the cookies on a cool, dry day. In hot, humid weather, meringue doesn't dry properly.

TOOLBOX

- ° 6 eggs
- ° cookie sheet and wax paper
- ° bowls
- ° ¼ teaspoon cream of tartar or white vinegar
- ° ½ cup sugar
- ° ¼ teaspoon vanilla extract

Caution: This activity involves using an electric mixer and an oven, so ask an adult to help.

▶ **Take the eggs out of the refrigerator and let them sit on the counter for about an hour or two until they come to room temperature.** Preheat the oven to 250 degrees Fahrenheit (121 degrees Celsius) and put the oven rack in the middle of the oven. Line a cookie sheet with wax paper.

▶ **Hold an egg lightly with one hand, and with the other hand, crack the eggshell firmly with a table (blunt) knife.** Pull the egg apart over a small metal or glass bowl, without letting the yolk break or fall into the bowl. Pour the yolk back and forth between the eggshell halves and let the egg white fall into the bowl. When all the white is in the bowl, put the yolk into another small bowl. You can save the yolks for another cooking project or throw them away. Now, pour the white from the small bowl into a larger glass or metal bowl, so that if you break a yolk in another egg, you won't ruin the whole batch.

❯ **Repeat step 2 with all the eggs.** Don't let any yolk get into the egg whites. When the egg whites are all in the large bowl, add the cream of tartar or white vinegar. Beat the mixture with an electric mixer on high until the egg whites get foamy and form soft peaks that gently flop over when you remove the beaters.

❯ **Gradually add the sugar and vanilla extract** and keep beating just until the meringue is shiny, smooth, and stands up in a peak about 2 inches high.

❯ **Drop big blobs of the meringue onto the wax paper on the cookie sheet and bake for 1 hour 30 minutes.** The meringues should look dry, stiff, and very light brown. Turn off the oven and let the meringue cookies cool completely in the oven before you take them out—at least 1 hour.

❯ **Clean up carefully!** You don't get to lick the bowl in this recipe because raw eggs can make you sick. For the same reason, make sure you use paper towels to wipe up any spilled raw egg, then throw them in the trash.

WHAT'S HAPPENING?

Egg whites are mostly water—about 88 percent. The rest is almost all protein, which is a polymer. The protein molecules are tightly wound, a bit like a slinky toy. When you whip the egg whites, the proteins unfold and stretch, forming a network of bubbles. Cream of tartar and vinegar are **acids** that help the egg whites unwind. As you whip the egg whites even more, the proteins begin to overlap, forming a long, stretchy surface. Eventually, the structure becomes more rigid. This is what makes the egg whites form stiff peaks. The heat from the oven "sets" the egg whites—the proteins unite and the structure becomes even more rigid.

Try This!

Try the recipe different ways. What happens if you use eggs that are right out of the refrigerator and still cold? What if you add lots and lots of sugar? What if you leave out the cream of tartar (or vinegar)? Remember, make one change at a time so you know which change made the difference and record your findings in your science journal.

WORDS TO KNOW

acid: a substance that donates a hydrogen ion (H+) to another substance. Examples include vinegar and lemon juice.

Chapter 2

MIX IT UP WITH
MIXTURES

What happens when the molecules of one substance mix it up with the molecules of another substance? You get a new substance—a mixture—all because of chemistry!

A **pure substance** is one in which all the molecules are the same. For example, pure gold is just gold. Sugar is also only one kind of molecule. Most things aren't pure substances, though. Even the water you drink isn't pure. It has many other kinds of molecules in it besides H_2O, such as fluoride, which is sometimes added to help make your teeth stronger. Pure is good, but things get a lot more interesting when pure substances are combined to make mixtures. A mixture is just that—a substance that has different materials mixed together. In some mixtures, you can see the different parts, similar to a bucket of pebbles with all different sizes and colors mixed together.

ESSENTIAL QUESTION

How are mixtures different from pure substances?

Look closely at a piece of wood. Do you see light and dark parts? Can you think of other mixtures you can see? For most mixtures, you can't see the different parts because they are mixed as molecules, which are too small to be visible. The molecules aren't bonded together. They are simply side by side—next to each other.

Imagine a huge room full of people. Some of the people are wearing white shirts—we'll call these white atoms. Others are wearing red shirts—red atoms. Each white atom has locked its arms, or bonded, with two red atoms, and all these groups are moving around the room. Sometimes, the groups bump into each other, but they don't unlock their arms or join arms with anyone else. Each group is a molecule and all the molecules are the same, so the room is a pure substance.

WORDS TO KNOW

mixture: a substance that has two or more different kinds of materials mixed together but not bonded together. Mixtures are easily separated into their parts.

pure substance: a substance, such as pure gold or a quartz crystal, where all the molecules are the same.

solution: the result when one substance has dissolved into another.

dissolve: when molecules of one substance get mixed into the molecules of another substance.

alloy: a substance made of two or more metals or of a metal and a nonmetal that are united (usually by melting them together).

corrosion: the wearing away of metal by a chemical reaction. Rust is a type of corrosion.

Solutions

A special kind of mixture is a **solution**. All mixtures are made up of two or more different kinds of molecules. Sometimes, you can see the different components, such as a mixture of sand and water. But sometimes, you can't see the different components and they're evenly distributed, such as salt in water or lemonade. This type of mixture is called a solution.

You might think that all solutions are a liquid and something **dissolved** in it. But solutions can also be two solids mixed together—called **alloys** when there are two metals mixed together. Alloys are important because they're used in making metals that are stronger, or cheaper, or resist **corrosion**. Steel, brass, and bronze are all alloys. Without alloys, we wouldn't have skyscrapers, jet airplanes, or automobiles!

KITCHEN CHEMISTRY

WORDS TO KNOW

magnetic: capable of attracting metal.

compound: a substance made up of two or more elements that are bonded together and not easily separated. Water is a compound.

evaporate: to convert from a liquid to a gas.

Now, imagine two kinds of groups. Some groups are the same as before, one white atom and two red atoms. Other groups are just two white atoms with their arms locked together. Each group is a molecule, but even though the same atoms are used, the molecules aren't the same. The room is a mixture.

Check out some delicious mixtures in this video!

🔎 TED-Ed macaroni mixtures

When substances are mixed together, their properties change, sometimes unexpectedly. Steel can be made harder or more flexible, depending on what other materials are mixed in. Adding salt to water makes it taste different and also makes it freeze at a lower temperature. Can you think of other mixtures that change the properties of a material? Mixtures can be solid, liquid, or gas. Without mixtures, we wouldn't have ice cream, grass, stars, life, or even chocolate!

SCIENCE DETECTIVES ARE ON THE CASE

Chemists are detectives. They figure out what's in stuff, how that stuff changes, and why. When chemists have a material and they don't know what it is, the first thing they do is separate the mixture into pure substances. Then, they figure out what the pure substances are.

A mixture of iron and sulfite. The iron was separated out from the sulfite with a magnet—iron is **magnetic**, but sulfite isn't!
credit: Asoult (CC BY 4.0)

Some Mixtures Are Yummy

Some mixtures are simple. Salt water is just water molecules with sodium chloride, or salt, mixed in. A penny is zinc and copper mixed together. Chocolate looks simple—it's all one color, the same texture, and it seems to melt all at once. You might think it's all made up of one type of molecule, maybe even called the "chocolate molecule." Or perhaps it's a simple mixture of two types of molecules. Chocolate is anything but simple, though. A study of one type of chocolate found 57 different **compounds** in it. That means this yummy chocolate bar has 57 different types of molecules all mixed up together. It's that complex mixture that gives chocolate its delicious, rich taste.

But how do you know if something is a mixture? It's easy when you can see the different parts, such as a mixture of pebbles that are different sizes. Often, though, something looks like it's a pure substance when it's really a mixture.

Try this: Pour some whole milk into a cup and let it sit on the counter for three or four days. After several days, look carefully at the milk. Can you see small white blobs? Milk might look like a pure substance, but to a chemist, it's not pure. It's a mixture! The white blobs you see are fat particles that are separating from the rest of the milk mixture. Don't forget to throw out the spoiling milk—yuck.

How can we separate out the different parts of a mixture? Some of the ways chemists separate out mixtures are by color, shape, size, density, or the temperature at which the parts melt or **evaporate**. Any difference between the different parts can be used.

STEEL is an ALLOY OF IRON and other elements, such as carbon. The amount of CARBON is small—usually only 2 percent or less—but it makes a big difference. Steel is much STRONGER THAN IRON!

CHEMISTRY DETECTION

Let's take a look at a time when scientists were called to solve a real chemistry mystery! The two parts of the mystery were separated by 26 years. It all began in the middle of the night on August 18, 1961, when people living in the coastal town of Capitola, California, woke to hear thousands of birds slamming into the walls of their homes. They rushed outside with flashlights, but the birds flew toward the lights, pecking at the people and sending them back inside, horrified. By dawn, the streets were covered with dead and stunned birds, and no one knew why.

Then, 26 years later, another mysterious incident happened, this one on the Atlantic coast of Canada. More than 100 people got very sick after eating mussels, a type of shellfish. A team of more than 40 scientists gathered to solve what came to be called the "amnesic shellfish poisoning mystery."

The mussel samples were a mixture of thousands of different chemical compounds, and scientists didn't even know what many of them were. How can you separate out an unknown chemical when you don't know what you're looking for or what its properties are?

Staff Sgt. Ashley Delcambre collects mussels for testing in California.
credit: U.S. Air Force photo by Airman 1st Class Ian Dudley/Released

ALFRED HITCHCOCK (1899–1980), a famous movie director, heard about the ill-fated birds. Two years later, he made a thriller film called *The Birds*, which featured an invasion of attacking birds.

Do you ever play the game 20 questions? You try to figure out what someone else is thinking. You start by asking about big categories, such as whether the unknown is a plant or an animal. Then, you keep narrowing things down until you know what it is.

The scientists knew the poison was affecting the **nervous system**. They couldn't test the poison on people, but they discovered that small amounts of it injected into mice caused them to scratch themselves. So, if the mice scratched themselves after being injected, that would be like getting a "yes" to one of the 20 questions. The scientists separated the mixture based on certain properties and injected each part into the mice to see which made the mice scratch.

For example, some compounds will dissolve in water and others in fat. One of the 20 questions was, "Does the poisoning agent dissolve in water or fat?"

Read an article and listen to the story of how scientists investigated the mystery of the Capitola birds.

KQED Santa Cruz

PS

WORDS TO KNOW

chromatography: a method of separating the components of a mixture by differences in their attraction to a liquid or gas.

algae: a plant-like organism that lives in water and grows by converting energy from the sun into food.

organism: any living thing.

To get an answer, they shook one mussel sample with a mixture of water and another mussel sample with a mixture of fat and injected the water and fat parts into different mice. The part of the mussel that dissolved in the water still caused the mice to scratch themselves, but the part that dissolved in fat didn't. So, they knew they were looking for a chemical that dissolves in water.

Scientist divided the MUSSELS over and over using many different METHODS, including chromatography, which is similar to the project at the end of this chapter.

Finally, the scientists separated out of the mixture a pure substance that was the toxic compound: domoic acid. It had come from a type of **algae**, an **organism** that had built up in the mussels. It turned out that, 26 years earlier, the birds in Capitola, had eaten anchovies, which had high concentrations of domoic acid from eating toxic algae. So, the birds, like the people in Canada, had probably been poisoned by the same thing.

See photos of a red tide and learn more about it in this article.

🔎 Sea Grant red tide

Now that the mystery is solved and we know exactly what caused the problem, seafood can be checked for domoic acid to avoid any more poisonings. This toxic algae is sometimes called "red tide." Scientists can warn people not to eat seafood harvested from a red tide.

Mixtures are just one way of creating new substances out of collections of molecules. In the next chapter, we'll learn about another way.

ESSENTIAL QUESTION

How are mixtures different from pure substances?

LEAVES AND DIRT
TRICK

TOOLBOX
- dry leaves
- dirt
- 2 bowls
- water
- 4 plates

Separating the parts of a mixture can be difficult, but there are some useful tricks. Try this one!

▶ **Mash up several dry leaves into little bits** and mix them with a handful of dirt in a deep bowl. Place half this mixture into another deep bowl.

▶ **Ask a friend or family member** if they would like to have a contest to see who can separate the dirt and leaves the fastest. Have someone time the contest.

▶ **Start the clock!** While your friend is frantically trying to separate the dirt and leaves, calmly pour water into the bowl. The dry leaves will float to the top, and the dirt will sink.

▶ **Scoop the leaves out onto a plate.** Pour off the water and scoop the dirt onto another plate. Ta-dah! You're the winner!

Colloids . . . What??

Colloids are another special type of mixture. They might look like a solution (described on page 23), but they're a little bit different. A colloid is a mixture that has very small particles of one substance mixed into another, but they're not completely dissolved. You probably drink a colloid every day: milk! It has little blobs of butterfat that are mixed into water. Other examples are butter, jelly, mayonnaise, lotion, and shampoo. And the best one of all: whipped cream!

Think About It

Think of other mixtures around the house. Are there any that you might be able to separate? Think about properties you might use to separate mixtures, such as size, shape, color, density, magnetism, or temperature. How might you separate spaghetti from the water it was boiled in? How about separating marbles from sand? What about salt from salt water?

CHROMACOLOR
BOOKMARK

The colors in markers are actually a mixture of different colors, or pigments. **Our eyes see the pigments as one color because the pigment molecules are completely mixed together and we can't distinguish one molecule from another. But just as the molecules of each pigment have a different color, they have other characteristics that are different, too, such as their size and how well they cling to water. Let's separate the color mixture and see what we get!**

❯ **Cut a paper coffee filter or blotting paper into as large a rectangle as possible.** Using nonpermanent, dark-colored markers, mark dashed lines 1 inch from the bottom of the short side of the paper. Use a different color marker for each dash.

❯ **Lightly tape the top of the paper rectangle to the middle of a pencil.** Place the pencil across the top of a tall, clear jar or drinking glass so that the filter paper hangs down inside the glass.

❯ **Slowly fill the glass with water** until the bottom of the paper is in the water, but the dashed lines are out of the water.

❯ **Let the paper sit for 15 minutes, checking it several times.** When the water has spread to the top of the paper, take it out of the water and let it dry. What do you see?

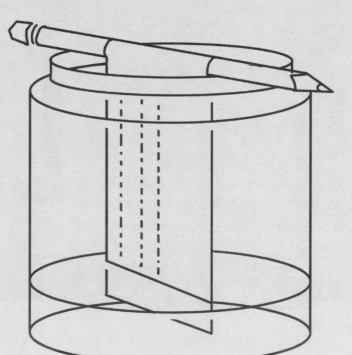

WORDS TO KNOW

pigment: a substance that gives color to something.

Chemical Signatures

Scientists use different types of chromatography as one way to figure out exactly what is in a substance. They use equipment that is more precise than your chromatography setup, but the principle is the same. Just as your signature looks different from everyone else's, each chemical has a "signature" that is different from other chemicals—it will travel along paper for a specific distance. Some substances can have hundreds of chemicals in them, and each chemical has a different signature.

> **If your colors all ended up near the top,** repeat steps 2 to 4, but take the paper out of the water sooner.

> **Cut out two pieces of cardstock so that they are a little larger than your filter paper.** Using a hole punch, punch holes through both pieces of cardstock at the same time. Make as many or as few holes as you like, but don't make them too close to the edge. You can make the holes in a design or just place them randomly.

> **Place the filter paper between the cardstock pieces** and tape the sides. You now have a stained-glass bookmark!

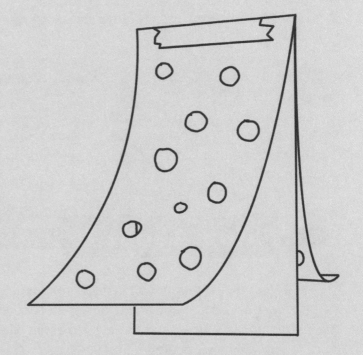

Try This!

Try the project again with light-colored markers. Do as many colors travel up the paper? What does that tell you about the types of molecules that are in different colored markers?

ONE PLUS ONE
EQUALS ONE

Try this activity to see how molecules in a solution mix together.

❯ **Place the pebbles or gravel into the large measuring cup to the one-cup mark.**

❯ **Pour 1 cup sand into the large measuring cup.** How much is the total of pebbles and sand? Record the amount in your science journal.

❯ **Pour 1 more cup of sand into the large measuring cup.** Record the total amount of pebbles and sand.

❯ **Empty the measuring cups and pour a quarter cup of water into the large measuring cup.**

❯ **Measure out a quarter cup of sugar, slowly pour it into the water, and stir.** Record the total amount of water and sugar. Keep pouring additional quarter cups of sugar, recording the total each time.

Think About It

Why does 1 cup of pebbles plus 1 cup of sand not total 2 cups in all? Where did the sand go? What about when you added another cup of sand; did that amount also "disappear"? What does this tell you about where the molecules of sugar might have gone when you poured it into the water?

You can't see the molecules of water or sugar, but they're a bit like the pebbles and sand. At first, the sugar molecules go in the spaces between the water molecules, like sand goes in the spaces between pebbles. But then the water is saturated, which means there are no more spaces for the sugar to fit into. The sugar won't dissolve anymore and the volume increases.

Chapter 3

REACTIONS:
PRESTO-CHANGE-O!

Have you ever watched a candle burn? That's a chemical reaction! A chemical reaction takes place when something changes into something else and can't be changed back. Reactions are the heart of chemistry. They might seem like magic, but reactions, as with everything in chemistry, happen for a reason.

In a chemical reaction, atoms are rearranged to make a new chemical substance. The materials you start with are called **reactants**, and the materials you end with are called **products**. For a reaction to occur, the bonds in molecules must break and then new bonds form.

ESSENTIAL QUESTION

Why does one chemical react with another?

Atoms bond to form molecules by trading or sharing electrons.

KITCHEN CHEMISTRY

Imagine again the room full of people wearing white shirts and red shirts—white atoms and red atoms—that we talked about in Chapter 2. The atoms lock arms and form bonds, creating molecules, only now they are in pairs of white-white and red-red.

Every time a white-white molecule and a red-red molecule collide, they break their bonds. Then, the white atoms form new bonds by locking arms and the red atoms form new bonds by locking arms.

This is like the bonds breaking in reactants and reforming to make a new kind of product. After all the molecules have had a chance to collide, the new white-red molecules would be the only type of molecule in the room. This new molecule would have different properties. A chemical reaction has taken place—maybe the new molecule will be pink!

Fire is the result of a chemical reaction!

Fireworks!

Have you ever seen fireworks at a baseball game or on the 4th of July? You're watching the results of a chemical reaction! Charcoal, sulfur, and potassium nitrate make up something called black powder, or gunpowder. Gunpowder is the earliest known chemical explosive, and it's still used today. A fuse lights gunpowder that blasts a metal tube up into the sky—as fast as a jet fighter! Once the tube is high in the air, more gunpowder inside the tube causes the firework to explode . . . bang!

When metal salts are burned, they give off a color. Different metal salts are added to fireworks to give different colors.

WHAT CAUSES REACTIONS?

Not all molecules react when they come into contact with each other. Whether an atom bonds with another atom—and the strength of that bond—depends on the number and arrangement of its electrons and how well they match up with the other atom's electrons.

To understand, let's review the structure of the atom you learned about in Chapter 1. Atoms have protons and neutrons clumped together in the nucleus, with electrons orbiting around the outside. Electrons move in **shells**, or regions of space, arranged a little bit like the rings of an onion.

The innermost, or first, shell can hold one or two electrons, the second shell can hold up to eight electrons, the third shell can hold up to 18 electrons, and so on. The innermost shells are always filled up before electrons are added to the next outer shell.

A **NUCLEUS** has up to seven of these **SHELLS** around it, with each holding a certain **NUMBER OF ELECTRONS.**

KITCHEN CHEMISTRY

It's the outermost shell that determines whether an atom will bond with another atom. Atoms are the most stable when their outer shells are full. If the outer shell is full, an atom does not bond easily with another atom. But if the outer shell is one or two electrons short of being full, the atom is unstable. It will react easily by grabbing an electron from somewhere else.

Where will the atom find an extra electron? From another atom that has just one electron in its outer shell, which means it is also unstable. When an atom gets rid of that extra electron hanging in a shell by itself, the shell underneath, which is full, becomes the outermost shell and it is then stable.

The periodic table of elements gives us some clues about which atoms are stable and unstable. Look back at the table on page iv. Hydrogen, with a symbol of H, has the atomic number 1. It has one proton and one electron, and it's in Group 1. Elements in Group 1 have an electron sitting all by itself in the outermost shell—not stable. These atoms easily give up that electron, leaving a stable shell underneath, or they share it with another atom. Now, look at oxygen on the right side of the periodic table, with a symbol of O and an atomic number of 8. It's in Group 16. All the elements in Group 16 have an outermost shell that is almost full—they're missing just two electrons.

Water is the result of a chemical reaction!

Here's an interactive periodic table. Click on an element and find out more about it. Keep in mind this chart was created before some of the elements we know today were discovered. NOVA also has an app, called NOVA Elements, that you can download to a smartphone.

🔍 NOVA periodic table

These atoms like to form bonds where they can grab or share two electrons from other atoms. If one oxygen atom, which needs two electrons, and two hydrogen atoms, each of which wants to give up one electron, bond together, they'll both be happy. Which is exactly what happens when water forms—H_2O.

FAST AND SLOW

Some reactions happen very fast. If you combine vinegar with baking soda it immediately bubbles up. Other reactions happen very slowly. Some examples of reactions you might see or know about around you are a nail rusting, a candle burning, **photosynthesis**, silver **tarnishing**, and yeast making bread rise.

For a reaction to occur, the reactants must physically come into contact with each other. In our imaginary room of white and red molecules, each molecule must bump into another before the bonds break and reform. Anything that makes the reactants come into contact more often will increase how fast the reaction happens.

A nail rusting reacts TOO SLOWLY for you to see it happen, ESPECIALLY in a dry climate.

What makes molecules come into contact more often? Higher temperatures, for one. At high temperatures, molecules move faster, so they'll be more likely to bump into each other. Another factor is the size of the particles of reactants. Powders, for example, react faster than a big hunk of a reactant. That's because powders have a much larger **surface area**, which means more area is available for contact with the other reactants. Have you ever stirred something before baking it? You're helping to mix together the molecules, which makes the reaction faster. Baking is all about chemical reactions!

WORDS TO KNOW

heat: the total energy from the motion of all the particles in a substance.

exothermic reaction: a chemical reaction that releases energy, usually in the form of heat. An example is a burning log.

endothermic reaction: a chemical reaction that absorbs energy. An example is photosynthesis in plants, which absorbs energy from the sun.

activation energy: the energy that starts a chemical reaction.

spontaneous: something that happens by itself without an apparent cause.

ENERGY

Reactions involve changes in energy. Some reactions give off energy, usually in the form of **heat**, and they're called **exothermic reactions**. Combustion, or burning, is the best example of an exothermic reaction. If you stand next to a bonfire, you can feel that the reaction of wood and oxygen is giving off energy.

Endothermic reactions absorb energy, or heat. When baking soda and vinegar react, the reaction absorbs energy, and you can measure that by taking the temperature before and after the reaction.

Photosynthesis is another endothermic reaction— plants absorb energy to make the reaction happen. Do you know where plants get the energy for photosynthesis?

Most chemical reactions are EXOTHERMIC, giving off HEAT.

IT'S HARD TO GET STARTED

Most reactions need a little boost of energy to get going, just like some people need a cup of coffee or tea in the morning to start their day. You know that a log of wood can burn. But, it needs a boost of energy or heat, such as a match, to get it started. Once it catches fire, the log will burn by itself. That extra energy that's needed to get a reaction started is called the **activation energy**. It's a good thing most reactions need activation energy or things would start burning all by themselves!

Some reactions are **spontaneous**, though. A spontaneous reaction doesn't need anything to get it started, it just happens. Rust is a good example. If all the chemical reactants are present, iron will rust without any activation energy.

Sometimes, it looks like a material has undergone a **REACTION**, but it hasn't. When water freezes or boils, it's just changing from a **LIQUID** to a **SOLID** or **GAS**. It's still the same molecule—H_2O. When chocolate melts in your hand, it's not reacting, it's just changing from a **SOLID** to a **LIQUID**.

Airbag Instant Pillow

Ever wonder how a giant pillow of air can come shooting out of such a small space in your car? Because of a chemical reaction, of course—actually, a whole string of them. An unused airbag has different chemicals in it, which are ignited by an electrical impulse that is triggered when the car stops very suddenly. One of these chemicals is sodium azide. Once ignited, sodium azide decomposes, or breaks down, into sodium and nitrogen gas. The nitrogen gas, which takes up more space, quickly fills the airbag.

KITCHEN CHEMISTRY

WORDS TO KNOW

base: a substance that accepts hydrogen from another substance. Examples include baking soda and ammonia.

alkaline: having a pH greater than 7.

pH: a measure of acidity or alkalinity, on a scale from 0 (most acidic) to 14 (most alkaline).

neutral: a liquid that is neither an acid nor a base.

fermentation: a chemical reaction that breaks down food.

neutralization: a reaction between an acid and a base that uses up all the acid and base. The products of the reaction are water and a salt with a neutral pH of 7.

ACIDS AND BASES

A special kind of reaction comes from acids and **bases**. Try to take a big bite out of a lemon without puckering your lips! That sour taste comes from the acid in the lemon juice. Acids can be found in other fruits as well, including limes, oranges, and grapes. The acids in these fruits and many other foods are weak acids and help give foods flavor. Strong acids, such as battery acid, are dangerous. These can damage your skin.

The opposite of an acid is a base, or **alkaline** substance. Weak bases, such as baking soda, taste bitter. Strong bases, such as oven cleaner, are dangerous and should never be tasted.

We use the **pH** scale to measure how acidic or basic a substance is. Acids and bases are on opposite sides of the pH scale. An acid has a pH between 0 and 7, and a base has a pH between 7 and 14. A pH of 7 is **neutral**.

Pickles

Your refrigerator probably contains a result of a chemical reaction—pickles! For thousands of years, people around the world have soaked vegetables or meats in salt or vinegar solutions to keep them from spoiling. The pickles in your refrigerator started as cucumbers. Cucumbers are soaked in a salty water and sealed off from the air. In a chemical reaction called **fermentation**, bacteria eat the sugars in the cucumbers and produce lactic acid. Fermentation also happens when you make bread. Yeast and bacteria take the sugars in the dough and produce carbon dioxide. That's what causes the little bubbles of gas that makes dough rise!

Rubidium

Rubidium (Rb) is a soft, silvery metal that is highly reactive—meaning it reacts easily with many elements. How reactive? It will burst into violent flames when exposed to water, creating an explosion of hydrogen gas. It will even spontaneously catch fire in air because of the water vapor in air. Like other elements in its group in the periodic table of elements, it has one lone electron in its outermost shell. You might think that any element unstable enough to set water on fire would react with anything. Strange as it sounds, rubidium is sometimes stored in kerosene, which is quite flammable. But kerosene doesn't react with rubidium, because it doesn't want that extra electron in the outer shell!

pH	Examples of solutions
0	Battery acid, strong hydrofluoric acid
1	Hydrochloric acid secreted by stomach lining
2	Lemon juice, gastric acid, vinegar
3	Grapefruit juice, orange juice, soda
4	Tomato juice, acid rain
5	Soft drinking water, black coffee
6	Urine, saliva
7	"Pure" water
8	Sea water
9	Baking soda
10	Great Salt Lake, milk of magnesia
11	Ammonia solution
12	Soapy water
13	Bleach, oven cleaner
14	Liquid drain cleaner

The pH scale
credit: OpenStax College

When an acid and a base—such as vinegar and baking soda—come together, they react, or change. When an acid and a base combine, they form water and a salt. The acid donates a proton, or hydrogen ion, and the base accepts it. If all the ions from the acid and the base are used up, then the final solution is neutral and the reaction is called a **neutralization.** Sometimes, either more of the acid or of the base is left, and not all of the reactants are neutralized. In this case, the final solution has water, a salt, and some of the excess acid or base.

Now that we know what matter is made of and how it forms other matter, let's take a closer look at some of the properties of solids.

ESSENTIAL QUESTION

Why does one chemical react with another?

41

RUSTY
SHAPES

TOOLBOX
- 4 glass jars
- salt
- plain steel wool without detergent
- cooking oil
- food thermometer
- science journal

Rust is a common chemical reaction. Iron and steel (which contains iron) rust in the presence of water and oxygen. The iron atoms in the metal bond with oxygen atoms to form iron oxide, or rust. The water acts as a bridge to transfer the electrons. Do this experiment and see for yourself!

❯ **Pour water into three glass jars, about half full.** Leave one jar dry. Add about a tablespoon of salt to one of the jars with water and stir. Label the jar.

❯ **Wash some plain steel wool (without a detergent coating) with dish detergent to remove any oil coating.** Rinse thoroughly and dry. Divide the steel wool pad into fourths. Pull each piece into a different shape, such as a star, a triangle, or an animal. Put one shape into each water-filled jar and the last one into the fourth empty jar. If necessary, add more water to cover the steel wool in the jars with water.

❯ **Slowly pour a layer of cooking oil about a half-inch thick over the plain water in one of the jars.** The oil will settle on the top.

❯ **Take the temperature of each piece of steel wool by inserting the thermometer into the middle of the steel wool for a minute.** Record the temperatures in your science journal, noting whether the steel wool measured was dry, under plain water, under salt water, or under water and oil. Make a prediction about whether the materials in any of the jars will undergo a reaction.

- water
- salt

- water

- water
- oil

- Empty

Salty

Salt is composed of sodium (Na) and chloride (Cl), with a formula of NaCl. When it dissolves in water, it separates into ions. Remember from Chapter 1 that an ion is an atom that has either gained or lost an electron and is either positively or negatively charged. Salt water has lots of positive ions (Na+) and negative ions (Cl-) in it and **corrodes** iron about 10 times faster than air.

❯ **Observe the jars a few hours later.** Do you see any change in the color of the steel wool? Record the temperature of each piece of steel wool again and compare them with the beginning temperatures. Have any of them changed?

❯ **Observe the jars a day later.** Do you see more changes? Which jar has changed the most? Which has changed the least? What reasons can you think of to explain these different changes? You can keep the experiment going as long as you like or pull out the shapes and attach them to a thread to make an ornament. Keep track of your observations in your science journal.

Think About It

What evidence do you have that a reaction has taken place? Pay special attention to appearance and temperature. Do you think the reaction is exothermic or endothermic?

WORDS TO KNOW

corrode: to wear away metal by a chemical reaction.

NAKED
EGGS

TOOLBOX
° a few eggs
° shallow dish or baking pan
° vinegar

What do you think happens when vinegar and eggshells come into contact? Let's do an experiment to find out!

❯ **Place a few whole eggs, still in their shells, in a shallow dish.** Try to keep the eggs from touching each other. Fill with enough vinegar to cover the eggs. Eggshells are made mostly of calcium carbonate. Calcium carbonate is a base, and its chemical symbol is $CaCO_3$. Dip your finger into the vinegar and taste it. Acidic foods taste sour and basic foods taste bitter. Do you think vinegar is an acid or a base?

❯ **Set the dish where you can see it but it will be undisturbed.** You can cover it if the vinegar smell bothers you. What do you think will happen when the eggshell soaks in the vinegar? Record your prediction in your journal.

❯ **After a day, carefully take out the eggs.** What do they look like? If the eggs aren't soft, pour out the old vinegar, put the eggs back in the shallow dish, and cover with new vinegar for another day. You may also see a chalky white layer on the outside of each egg. If the egg is soft, you can gently rub off this remnant of the shell under running water.

❯ **Hold a naked egg a few inches above the kitchen sink and drop it.** How far can you drop an egg before it breaks? Can you gently squeeze your egg? If the egg breaks, be sure to wash your hands thoroughly with soap and water. Try doing the same experiment with hard-boiled eggs. (Ask an adult to help you boil the eggs.) Are there any differences?

Think About It

Did the shell actually disappear? Not exactly—it changed. The calcium carbonate molecules that make up the shell break up in the reaction with the vinegar and form new molecules, or products. The products of the reaction are carbon dioxide, calcium acetate, and water. The calcium acetate and water are in the vinegar solution, and the carbon dioxide is a gas—it makes bubbles. Look closely at the surface of the eggs. Do you see bubbles? Under the shell, the egg is encased in a thin membrane. This membrane becomes rubbery when it allows liquid to pass through it. That extra liquid, plus the flexible membrane, lets you bounce the egg. Watch out, though. If you bounce it too hard—splat!

WORDS TO KNOW

climate change: the long-term change in temperature and weather patterns across a large area, in particular attributed to the use of fossil fuels as an energy source.

adapt: to make a change in response to new or different conditions.

Coral reefs

Just like eggshells, seashells, pearls, limestone, and chalk are made of calcium carbonate. So are some of the most beautiful and complex places on earth—coral reefs.

Organisms called corals build coral reefs. Corals take calcium and carbonate ions in seawater and make

calcium carbonate skeletons. The ocean is naturally basic, with a pH a little above 8. When the pH is lowered, even if it's still somewhat basic, not as many carbonate ions are floating around, and it's harder for corals to make their skeletons. Without enough raw materials, the corals can't work efficiently.

What can lower the pH of an entire ocean? An acid! The earth's atmosphere naturally contains a small amount of carbon dioxide. Carbon dioxide in the atmosphere isn't an acid, but when it dissolves in water, it makes a weak acid called carbonic acid.

The pH of shallow waters in the ocean before the Industrial Revolution was about 8.15, but due to **climate change**, the pH is now about 8.05. That's a small change, but it's enough to mean lower concentrations of carbonate ions. Corals can still make their skeletons, but it's more difficult and they now are more sensitive to other stresses, such as pollution. The ocean may not always be alkaline enough for corals. Scientists are researching the complex interactions between the atmosphere, the ocean, and coral reefs so we can work to make sure corals have what they need to live and grow.

See a coral farm in the Bahamas that helps corals grow 50 times faster than in nature, to help them **adapt** more quickly to warming and more acidic oceans.

 Yale coral farm

CLEAN
PENNIES

TOOLBOX

- ° vinegar
- ° 2 bowls
- ° salt
- ° several pennies, some before 1982
- ° toothpicks
- ° brass washers and nuts
- ° science journal
- ° embroidery thread

❱ **Pour vinegar into two bowls, enough to cover the bottom.** Add about a spoonful of salt to each bowl and stir well. Place several pennies (some marked with a date before 1982 if possible) into each bowl, keeping one penny aside. Hold the extra penny halfway in the vinegar for about a minute. Do you see a difference in the two halves of the penny?

❱ **Insert a toothpick through the holes of several brass washers and nuts, alternating the washers and nuts.** Set the toothpick into one of the bowls so that the washers and nuts are half in the vinegar-salt solution and half in the air.

❱ **After about 10 minutes, look at the pennies in each bowl.** Do the pennies look different? Take the pennies out of the bowl without the washers and nuts.

❱ **After about a day or two, take out the rest of the pennies, washers, and nuts.** When the objects are dry, look at them closely. Did your washers, nuts, and pennies change color? Where do you think the color came from? Is there a difference between pennies dated before 1982, which are solid copper, and newer pennies, which have just a coating of copper?

❱ **To make a necklace, cut some embroidery thread about 18 inches long.** String the washers and nuts on the thread, alternating washers and nuts. Tie the thread in a knot. You can also use washers and nuts that were not placed in the solution for a silver-color contrast.

Think About It

Pennies are either made of or coated with copper, a pure substance that is very shiny. But, as time passes, the copper atoms on pennies combine with oxygen atoms in the air to form copper oxide, which gives pennies a dull look. What do you think might be happening when you place the pennies in the vinegar-and-salt solution? Why do you think you dissolved salt into the vinegar before putting in the pennies (look at a previous experiment, Rusty Shapes, for a clue)?

The washers and nuts are made of brass, which is a mixture of copper and zinc. Did they change appearance? Where do you think the color might have come from?

Chapter 4

SOLIDS:
IT'S A STATE OF MIND

Matter has three common states: solid, liquid, and gas. Plasma, an ionized gas, is considered a less common, fourth state of matter.

The **state of matter** affects the properties of a material, such as its fluidity or its density, but it doesn't affect the chemical makeup of the matter. For example, water can be a liquid, a solid (ice), or a gas (water vapor or steam). In all three cases, it's still made of H_2O molecules—the only difference is how those molecules are arranged.

Everybody knows what a solid is. It's hard, doesn't change its shape, and you can't pour it. But what about a handful of sand? A piece of soft fabric? They're solids, too. If you look at a small enough piece of a substance—a grain of sand—you can see that it holds its shape. Sand only pours because you have lots of little solid grains. And while fleece might feel soft, that's because the fabric is flexible. It bends, but it's still solid.

ESSENTIAL QUESTION

What makes a solid, a solid?

KITCHEN CHEMISTRY

To understand what makes something a solid, you have to look at the smallest parts—the atoms. The particles in solids are bound tightly into a particular shape. The atoms can still vibrate, similar to how a string on a violin vibrates, but they can't change places with each other. Because the atoms in solids stay in the same place, solids hold their shape and don't flow to fit a container. If you take a basketball and place it in a bucket, the basketball doesn't change its shape. A single grain of sand wouldn't change its shape to fit into a teeny tiny bucket!

Solids can have all sorts of different properties, such as strength, **hardness**, **elasticity**, and the ability to bend. Those properties are due to the arrangement of the atoms in a solid. Solids have less energy than liquids, which have less energy than gases.

Is that really a solid pouring over the elephant's back?

Solids can be as different as they are similar. Some solids are very hard, which means they aren't easily scratched, bent, or dented. Think of a rock— it's a solid that's quite hard. Now, think of a piece of chewing gum. That, too, is a solid, but it's not very hard, is it?

What about a rubber band? It's a solid, but it can stretch. It has elasticity, or the ability to bounce back to its original shape. Not similar at all to a rock! And all solids have their own measure of strength, or how much force they can withstand before crumpling or breaking. Under the umbrella category of solid, objects can be widely different.

When a solid is heated, its atoms vibrate faster and faster, with more and more energy. When the vibration becomes strong enough, the atoms break away from each other. This is called the **melting point**, and when this happens, the solid becomes a liquid— which is the topic of our next chapter!

It might seem that all solids share many of the same properties, but let's take a look at some different types of solids.

Some solids are malleable. This means they can be SQUASHED into many different shapes without breaking. The opposite of malleable is BRITTLE. Brittle objects break and split instead of changing shape.

WORDS TO KNOW

crystal: a solid with its atoms arranged in a geometric pattern.

geometric arrangements: crystal systems, or ways in which crystals are arranged.

amorphous solid: a solid where the atoms are in a mostly random, but still tightly bonded, arrangement.

CRYSTALS

Crystals are a special form of solid, where the atoms are arranged in an orderly pattern. If you think of an entire crystal as a building, then the building blocks would be molecules. These building blocks are stacked up like bricks. If conditions are right, the building blocks stack up into a crystal big enough to see.

If you could shrink down to the size of an atom, you would see the regular arrangement of the atoms. But, in fact, you don't have to shrink down to see this—the shape of the big crystal is the same as the shape of the smaller, molecular building blocks.

Often, a solid is made up of many very small crystals packed together in a mass. In this case, the solid doesn't look like a crystal. Instead, it will have a rough surface.

There are only seven different types of crystal systems, or **geometric arrangements**, but there are many types of crystals. What makes the difference are the different atoms in each crystal. Blue sapphires and red rubies are the same kind of crystal, but sapphires have small amounts of iron and titanium, while rubies have small amounts of chromium.

Can you see the crystalline structure of this blue sapphire?

credit: James St. John (CC BY 2.0)

Is Glass Really a Solid?

You may have heard that glass is really a liquid that flows very, very slowly. The main "support" for this idea is window glass in old cathedrals and other buildings from the Middle Ages that seems to have deformed, or flowed, over time. The glass is often thicker at the bottom of the window. It turns out, though, that the glass was probably made unevenly, since glassmaking techniques weren't very advanced back then. Today, glass is very even in thickness, and experiments don't show glass flowing, even after long periods of time. In fact, glass made during the ancient Roman era hasn't deformed through many centuries. Just to confuse matters, though, glass does have some properties of liquids, mainly its random arrangement of atoms, so some scientists think of glass as its own state of matter, neither liquid nor solid.

AMOR . . . WHAT?

Look out your window. You're looking through an **amorphous solid**—or glass, as it's more commonly known. Amorphous solids are the opposite of crystal solids. The word "amorphous" means without a definite structure, or disorganized.

If you think of a crystal as having particles arranged like eggs in a carton all lined up, then an amorphous solid would be like having particles arranged like marbles in a jar—a big jumble. The particles are arranged randomly,

The plastic in sandwich bags is an AMORPHOUS SOLID.

as in a liquid, but they're still tightly bound—they can't change places or flow around each other.

WORDS TO KNOW

fulgurite: often tubular glass that forms when lightning strikes sand.

semiconductor: a material that conducts some electricity.

impurity: contamination or pollution.

Amorphous solids can form from liquids that cool very quickly—for example, when hot lava cools into volcanic glass. As a liquid cools, the molecules lose energy and move more and more slowly. As the liquid turns into a solid, the molecules normally settle into an orderly arrangement, or crystal. But, if the liquid cools very quickly, the atoms do not have time to arrange themselves and they bond in a more random arrangement.

Many solids are a combination of crystalline and amorphous structures. Wood, for example, has areas with an orderly arrangement of atoms and other areas with randomly arranged atoms.

Solids are pretty fascinating, and they get even more interesting when you apply heat and a solid turns into a liquid! We'll learn more in the next chapter.

Fulgurite is a special kind of glassy tube that forms when LIGHTNING STRIKES sand. The intense heat fuses the grains of sand together—pow!

ESSENTIAL QUESTION

What makes a solid, a solid?

Silicon is Special

Silicon is the second most abundant element in the earth's crust, after oxygen. More than 90 percent of the earth's crust is composed of minerals with silicon in them. But, if you look on the periodic table, you can see something else. Silicon, with a symbol of Si and an atomic number of 14, is located in a diagonal row of elements that are **semiconductors**. Semiconductors are incredibly useful because their electrical properties can be controlled by adding small amounts of **impurities**. That may not sound very exciting, but without semiconductors, we wouldn't have laptop computers, cell phones, flat-screen televisions, satellites, or most modern medical equipment. Silicon is the main component of semiconductor chips used in electronics.

MAKE YOUR OWN
CRYSTALS

Grow your own salt crystals in this experiment!

> **Caution:** This project involves boiling water, so ask an adult to help.

❯ **Place a few salt grains (sodium chloride) onto black paper or a dark surface and look at the grains closely, using a magnifying glass if you have one.** What shape are the grains? Draw a picture in your science journal. You'll compare this salt to the crystals you grow.

❯ **Cut some cotton string into about eight pieces, each about 6 inches long.** Tie the strings together at one end. Boil about 2 cups of water in a saucepan. (Make sure you have an adult help with this part.)

❯ **Stir in salt slowly, 1 teaspoon at a time.** Mix well each time. Continue adding salt until it won't dissolve anymore and the salt starts to collect on the bottom of the pot. If you want colored crystals, add food coloring.

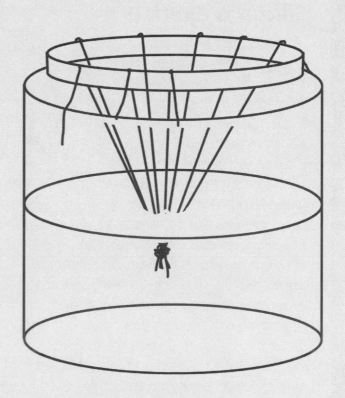

❯ **Allow to cool for a minute, then carefully pour about half of the solution into a shallow pan and the other half into a glass jar.** Do not allow any of the undissolved salt to get into the jar or pan.

❯ **Place the strings into the jar, with the knotted end submerged in the salt solution.** Let the other ends drape over the rim of the jar.

❯ **Move the pan and jar to a dark location where they won't be disturbed.** Place paper towels under the jar to catch any drips from the strings. If the level of the solution goes below the knot, add more salt solution, prepared as before.

❯ **What happens?** The salt crystals should start forming in about a day. The slower the crystals grow, the larger they will be. Leave the solution for about two weeks, checking each day. Record your observations in your science journal.

Try This!

Look at the crystals closely. How are they different from the original salt crystals? How are they the same? Do the crystals forming in the pan look different from the ones on the strings? Try the same experiment with different lengths of string, in different arrangements or shapes. Can you make a string salt sculpture?

WHAT'S HAPPENING?

Table salt, or sodium chloride, is a crystal solid—the sodium and chloride atoms are arranged in a particular order. When you add salt to water—a **solvent**—it becomes a solution. This means that the sodium and chloride atoms separate and are surrounded by water molecules. But, water can hold only certain amounts of a **solute** such as salt before it won't dissolve anymore. At this point, the solution is **saturated**. Hot water, however, can hold more salt than cold water, so when the water cools, it's holding more salt than normal. If it cools slowly and isn't disturbed, the salt can form into fairly big crystals.

WORDS TO KNOW

solvent: the substance that dissolves a solute.

solute: the dissolved substance in a solution.

saturated: a solvent that is no longer able to dissolve any more solute.

NEEDLE CRYSTALS

Now, try growing a different shape crystal.

❯ **Place a few Epsom salt grains (you can get Epsom salts from the pharmacy) on black construction paper and look at them closely.** Use a magnifying glass if you have one. What shape are the grains? How are they different from regular salt crystals?

❯ **Cut the paper into whatever shape you like, such as a snowflake or heart.** Place the paper on a cookie sheet with sides. Trim the paper if it doesn't fit completely within.

❯ **Pour about one cup of hot tap water into a bowl.** Slowly pour 1 cup of Epsom salts into the hot water, stirring constantly. Keep stirring until all the Epsom salts are dissolved, if possible. Add food coloring if you like.

EPSOM SALTS are used for healing cuts and shallow wounds. The mineral EPSOMITE, which is the same as Epsom salt, was first discovered near Epsom, England. Epsomite can be found encrusting limestone cave walls.

❯ **Pour the solution over the paper.** Place the cookie sheet with the paper and solution in a warm place, such as a sunny window. With an adult's help, you can also place the cookie sheet in a warm oven at about 200 degrees Fahrenheit (93 degrees Celsius) for 15 minutes or so, but watch it to make sure the paper doesn't dry out too much. You should start to see lots of large, spiky crystals growing. Record your observations in your science journal.

Think About It

How are the newly formed crystals different from the original, Epsom salt crystals? Why do you think the crystals look different?

MAKE YOUR OWN
SILLY GOOP

Try making some fun goop to see some surprising properties solids can have!

▶ **In a paper cup, mix the glue,** 4 tablespoons water, and a few drops of food coloring. Add 1 tablespoon borax and the cornstarch and mix well.

▶ **In another cup,** mix ⅔ cup water and 2 teaspoons borax until the borax dissolves. Pour 2 tablespoons of the borax-and-water solution into the glue mixture and stir until it's stiff.

▶ **Let the mixture set for a minute,** then take it out of the cup and rinse with water. Blot the extra water with a paper towel and knead the mixture until it's smooth. If you want it to be stiffer, add more of the borax-and-water solution. What does your silly goop do? Try bouncing it, breaking it, and stretching it. Does it keep its shape? Is it hard or soft or both?

WHAT'S HAPPENING?

The glue contains a polymer, which means it contains very long chains of molecules. The borax causes the chains to link to each other so that it sticks to you less and sticks more to itself. The molecules aren't in a fixed crystalline structure, so the goop can stretch as the molecules unwind and move past each other, but not as much as the liquid glue.

Try This!

Vary the amounts of the ingredients to make the goop more fluid or stiffer. Keep track of what you vary in your journal, and remember to change only one thing at a time.

Chapter 5

LIQUIDS:
GO WITH THE FLOW!

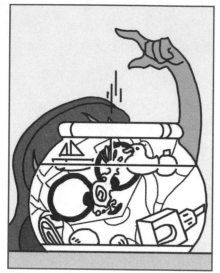

What shape is water? Milk? These liquids take the shape of whatever container you put them in! This is a primary characteristic of a liquid. Liquid flows because clusters of molecules can slide past each other. Molecules in a liquid have more energy than those in a solid, but less than those in a gas.

Most liquids have very different properties from solids. First, let's look at density. Density is the amount of **mass** in a certain volume. Remember, volume is the amount of space occupied by something. In general, solids are slightly denser than liquids and liquids are a lot denser than gases. Different liquids can have different densities, depending on their chemical makeup.

ESSENTIAL QUESTION

How are liquids important in everyday life?

Density increases in two ways. Either more mass (molecules) is added to the same amount of volume or the volume that contains the molecules is made smaller. The opposite actions decrease density.

If you add salt to water, the salt breaks apart and its particles slip into the spaces between the water molecules. The mass increases, but because the salt particles slipped into empty spaces, the volume doesn't increase—which makes salt water denser than fresh water. What if the same number of molecules are enclosed in a slightly larger volume? The liquid is less dense.

Heating a liquid makes it a bit less dense. With heat, the molecules move around faster, so there's a little more space between them. The same principles of density apply to solids and gases as well.

WORDS TO KNOW

mass: the amount of matter or "stuff" in something. On Earth, the mass of something is very close to its weight.

diplomat: a person who represents one country to another.

Benjamin Franklin

Benjamin Franklin was a great inventor and **diplomat**, as well as one of America's founding fathers. He was also a very curious person, which made him an excellent scientist. In 1757, when he was on a ship in a fleet traveling to America from England, he noticed that the ships at the end of the line sailed more smoothly than those in front. Of course, he wondered why. The ship's captain gave him a clue when he said, "The cooks have been just emptying their greasy water through the scuppers, which has greased the sides of those ships [at the end] a little." Franklin remembered this explanation about oil smoothing the water. One windy day, when he was back in London, England, he dropped about a teaspoon of oil into Clapham Pond and watched as it slowly spread out. Oil is less dense than water and floats on top. That little bit of oil kept spreading and spreading until it covered an area about as big as half a football field. Franklin said the oil made the water "as smooth as a looking glass." More than 100 years later, Lord Rayleigh (1842–1919), a famous scientist, built on Benjamin Franklin's experiments. He was able to calculate that when oil spread on water, it was a molecule thick.

WORDS TO KNOW

displace: to replace fluid with an object. The weight of the water moved equals the object's weight.

biodegrade: to break down or decay and become absorbed into the environment.

bacteria: tiny organisms found in animals, plants, soil, and water that help decay food. Some bacteria are harmful and others are helpful.

BCE: put after a date, BCE stands for Before Common Era and counts down to zero. CE stands for Common Era and counts up from zero. This book was printed in 2020 CE.

FLOATING AND SINKING

How is density important when you go swimming or boating? Have you ever kicked back in a refreshing lake or pool and felt the water lift you up? The water is pushing up against you, supporting some of your weight. What happens when you try to lift your head out of the water? You start to sink.

Whether something floats or sinks depends on its density. Something that is very dense sinks because it's heavier than the water it **displaces**. Your body is less dense than water, so you float.

Oil Spills

Sometimes, oil tankers or equipment holding oil can have an accident and the oil leaks out into the ocean. Because oil is less dense than water, the oil spreads and floats on top of the seawater. Birds and animals can become coated in the oil, and then they can't fly or stay warm. Oil takes a long time to break down, or **biodegrade**, into other substances, so it can have a terrible effect on wildlife.

To clean up an oil spill, workers first use booms, which are floating barriers that look like very long tube socks stuffed with material. The booms circle around the spill to keep it from spreading further. Sometimes, workers use a detergent that breaks up the oil into little droplets, which can help it biodegrade faster. But the little droplets can still hurt wildlife. Sometimes, workers use giant vacuums to suck up the oil or skimmers to skim the oil from the water's surface into big tanks. Sometimes, they use special absorbent materials that soak up the oil but not the water. And sometimes, they add **bacteria**! We sometimes think of bacteria as bad, but there's also good bacteria. Some bacteria can "eat" the oil and help to break it down into harmless substances—it's a chemical reaction!

It might not seem that a ship this large and heavy could float!

Big, steel ships don't look as though they could float! After all, they can weigh tens of thousands of tons. And steel is much denser than water. If you dropped a cube of steel into water, it would sink. But a steel ship floats because of its shape. The weight of the water that the ship's hull displaces equals the weight of the ship and the cargo combined. A ship also includes wood and air and people, which together have a lower density than water.

When you **LIFT** your head up, your **BODY** isn't displacing as much water, and you start to **SINK**.

EUREKA

More than 2,000 years ago, a Greek mathematician and scientist named Archimedes (228–212 **BCE**) was given the task of finding out if King Hiero's crown was pure gold. But he was not allowed to hurt the crown in any way in his pursuit of the truth.

WORDS TO KNOW

Archimedes' principle: when an object is placed in a fluid, it experiences an upward force that is equal to the weight of the fluid that is displaced.

buoyancy: the force that makes something able to float in a liquid or gas.

viscous: having a thick and sticky consistency. Honey is very viscous, while water is not.

resistance: a force that slows down another force.

refine: to purify a substance to make it usable for certain tasks.

Archimedes knew that different materials have different densities, so two different materials that weigh the same would have different volumes. Since the goldsmith had been given a specific weight of gold, the crown should have a specific volume. If the gold was mixed with silver, for example, the crown would have a greater volume because silver is less dense.

According to legend, Archimedes noticed the water overflowed as he stepped into the bath. The solution to the crown problem came to him: He could measure the exact volume of the crown by measuring the volume of water it displaced. If the crown was made of silver and gold together, it would displace more water than one made only of gold.

He was so excited that he ran naked into the street, yelling, "Eureka!" What he concluded is now known as **Archimedes' principle**. When an object is placed in a fluid, it experiences an upward force that is equal to the weight of the fluid that is displaced. Also known as the principle of **buoyancy**, it determines whether something sinks or floats.

VISCOSITY

Try pouring water into one glass and corn syrup or honey into another. Which takes longer to pour? In some liquids, the molecules find it harder to slide past each other. These liquids are more **viscous**, which means that they have more **resistance** to flow. The corn syrup is more viscous—sometimes we say that it is "thicker." Viscosity is important in industrial processes, such as **refining** and using oil.

Have you ever done an experiment that seemed to take forever? Perhaps you had to boil water or grow mold and you had to wait many long minutes or maybe even days. What if you had to wait years?

This liquid is more viscous than water.

Pascal's law: when a liquid or gas is pushed on by a force, it transmits the force to all parts of the fluid.

non-Newtonian fluid: a substance that can behave both like a solid and a liquid.

dilatant liquid: a liquid that flows more slowly when a force is applied.

suspension: a mixture made up of relatively large particles of a solid within a liquid. The particles settle out if the mixture is undisturbed.

In 1927, at the University of Queensland in Australia, Professor Thomas Parnell (1881–1948) started an experiment that's still going—the pitch drop. He wanted to prove that something that seems to be a solid can have liquid properties if you wait long enough. He used pitch, a substance made from tar, to do it. Pitch looks like a solid, feels like a solid, and if you strike it with a hammer, it shatters like a solid. But is it?

Parnell heated the pitch to make it flow and poured it into a sealed funnel. He let it cool and settle for three years, then took off the seal. Not much happened for a very long time—eight years, in fact. Although pitch looks like a solid, it flows like a liquid—only it flows very, very slowly. That's because it is extremely viscous—20 billion times more viscous than water. It took a full eight years for one single drop to fall through the funnel into the beaker below!

As of today, 93 years later, a total of only nine drops have fallen. Drops are taking even longer to fall now because air conditioning was installed in the building, which cools the pitch and makes it even more viscous.

Push!

When a liquid is pushed on by a force, the pressure from that force is the same throughout the liquid. This principle is called **Pascal's law**, and it also applies to gases. You see an example of this every day when you squeeze a tube of toothpaste. You squeeze on one end, but the pressure transmits throughout the paste, which is pushed out the opening. This principle is also used in the brakes in a car. Fluid is compressed in the brake pedal and is transmitted to the axle that is attached to the wheels. When you step on the brake, it stops the axle and wheels.

NON-NEWTONIAN FLUIDS

Have you ever made oobleck? This is the stuff made of water and cornstarch that seems like a liquid until you squeeze it or hit it. That's when it feels like a solid! A substance such as this is called a **non-Newtonian fluid**. Oobleck behaves differently when a force is applied to it. A liquid that flows more slowly when a force is applied is called **dilatant liquid**. The big question is why this happens.

The **PITCH DROP** experiment holds the Guinness World Record for the longest-running laboratory EXPERIMENT.

Believe it or not, scientists don't completely understand why, though they have some ideas. Oobleck is not a simple liquid, like water, but rather is a **suspension**. The particles of cornstarch don't dissolve in water the way salt does—tiny bits of solid cornstarch are still floating, or suspended, in the water. You can see this if you let the mixture sit for a while. The cornstarch settles to the bottom.

Trinity College in Dublin, Ireland, caught a drop of pitch falling on camera on July 11, 2013. **Check it out!**

🔎 nature pitch drop

The size of the cornstarch bits is an important part of why the oobleck suspension is dilatant. The cornstarch particles are all about the same size, a little smaller than the width of a human hair. When hit with a strong force, scientists think that the particles jam together into a cluster, like a log jam, and can't slip past each other. The tiny clusters prevent anything from getting through. But, when something moves slowly through oobleck, the particles have time to get out of the way and don't clump. You'll get a chance to see for yourself in an activity!

Now that you know many of the properties of liquids, we'll take look at another state of matter—gases!

ESSENTIAL QUESTION

How are liquids important in everyday life?

WAVE
TANK

Oil is more viscous than water—it flows more slowly—so it slows down the flow of the water. See for yourself!

❯ **Remove the labels from a 2-liter clear, plastic bottle.** Fill the bottle half full of water. Add a few drops of blue food coloring and one drop of green food coloring to the water. Screw on the lid and slowly tilt the bottle from side to side. Write down your observations in your science journal.

❯ **Add about ½ cup of mineral oil or baby oil to the bottle.** Let the water and oil settle.

❯ **Slip the piece of candle through the bottle opening into the water and oil.** Screw on the lid and tilt the bottle from side to side.

❯ **Look carefully at the oil and water.** Do they mix? Is the oil or the water on top? Where is the candle? What does that tell you about their densities? In your science journal, write down the order of densities of the candle, water, and oil.

Workers use absorbent pompoms to clean up an oil spill. It's very difficult to remove oil from large areas of water!

Try This!

Try tilting the bottle quickly and slowly, as well as doing big tilts and small tilts. Write down your observations or draw a picture in your science journal. How does this compare to how the liquid moved when it was just water?

LAYER CAKE
LIQUIDS

Explore materials of different densities in this experiment!

TOOLBOX
- honey or corn syrup
- tall, clear glass or jar
- water
- cup
- food coloring
- cooking oil
- rubbing alcohol
- several objects of different densities

❯ **Pour honey or corn syrup into the bottom of a tall, clear glass or jar until it is a little less than a quarter full.** Try not to let the honey touch the sides of the jar as you're pouring it.

❯ **Pour water into a separate cup.** Add a few drops of food coloring. Slightly tilt the jar and slowly pour the water into the jar, letting it run down along the side until it's about the same depth as the honey. If the liquids mix, let the jar sit for a minute until the liquids separate.

❯ **Using cooking oil instead of water, repeat step 2, without using food coloring.**

❯ **Using rubbing alcohol instead of water, repeat step 2, using a different color food coloring.** Which is the densest liquid? The least dense?

❯ **Select several objects that you think have different densities, such as a coin, grape, cork, raisin, ping pong ball, a Lego brick or other plastic piece, and aluminum foil.** Lower each object into the jar, being careful not to disturb the liquids. Which is the densest object? Record your observations in your science journal.

Try This!

Aluminum foil is a good material to help vary the density of objects. You can pound it into a little ball or shape it into a little cup. Is there a difference in where it floats or sinks? Think about the two shapes and how much liquid they replace. You can also use aluminum to wrap around two objects of different density to try to find objects that will float between different layers of the liquids. Record your findings.

OOBLECK

Some substances are still a mystery to us. Non-Newtonian fluids are one kind of these! To make your own non-Newtonian fluid, you just need cornstarch and water. Cornstarch is a polymer, which is a long molecule. When combined with water, it becomes a strange material that doesn't follow the same rules that many other materials do.

❱ **Spread newspaper over your workspace.** Put about 1 cup cornstarch into a bowl. Slowly add about ½ cup water, mixing with your fingers until all the cornstarch is wet. Add a few drops of food coloring if you like. Congratulations! You have just made oobleck!

❱ **Play with your oobleck.** You can adjust it by adding a little more cornstarch if it feels too wet or more water if it feels too powdery.

❱ **What happens if you squeeze the oobleck and then open your hand?** Try slapping the oobleck hard, then slowly sinking your fingers into it. How is this different from when you push hard on water? Make a ball or roll out a snake and see what happens when you stop rolling. Record your findings in your science journal.

Watch how people choose to tackle a pool of oobleck!

🔎 Mach Bank non-Newtonian fluid

PS

❱ **When you're done, put the oobleck in a trash can.** Never put it down the drain.

Try This!

With an adult's permission, take your oobleck to a dance party! Put the oobleck in a metal container and place it on top of a music speaker. Turn up the base and see what happens. Can you explain the oobleck's behavior?

Newton

Sir Isaac Newton (1642–1726) was a brilliant scientist who described how liquids flow. You'll read more about him in the next chapter on gases. He noted that liquids have a constant viscosity, or thickness, and that the viscosity changed only with changes in temperature or pressure. How fast it flows doesn't depend on the stress put on it. If you shake a glass of water, it doesn't flow faster or slower because of it.

Non-Newtonian liquids change how viscous they are when you apply stress. Some of them flow more easily and some become stiffer. Your kitchen has some non-Newtonian liquids, such as honey and ketchup. Try stirring them and see if they start to flow more easily or get stiffer.

This non-Newtonian fluid is reacting to sound waves from a speaker!
credit: Rory MacLeod (CC BY 2.0)

Chapter 6

GASES:
IT'S SOMETHING IN THE AIR

Some things in this world are invisible, even without a magic spell or invisibility cloak. Blow on your arm. Can you feel that? Even though you usually can't see gases because they're transparent and colorless, you can see or feel the effects they have.

ESSENTIAL QUESTION

Why does gas expand to fill a container?

Gases are one of the three states of matter, along with solids and liquids. Gases are much less structured than the other two, though, because they easily change both their volume and shape. A gas will not only flow like a liquid, it will also expand to fill a container.

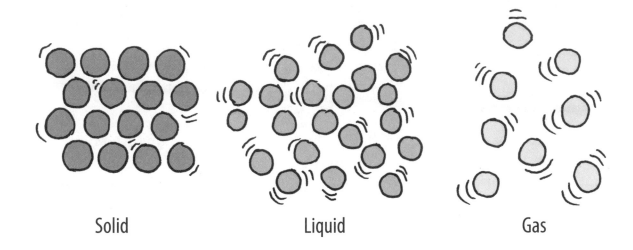

Solid   Liquid   Gas

RUNNING ON EMPTY

If you could shrink to the size of a molecule and float around in a gas, you would see mostly . . . nothing. About 99.96 percent of the total volume of gas is empty space. The molecules are very far apart relative to their size—but they do have lots of energy.

Gas molecules travel in a straight line until they run into another molecule or the sides of the container that they're in. Imagine a classroom of kids who have all just eaten lots and lots of candy and are bouncing off the walls and each other—except it's a very large classroom compared to the size of the kids.

On a warm day, **OXYGEN GAS MOLECULES** travel at an average speed of about 1,030 miles per hour. This is faster than a jet airplane. Those oxygen molecules don't cross a room very fast, though, because they each have about 5 or 6 billion crashes with other molecules in one second.

KITCHEN CHEMISTRY

WORDS TO KNOW

collide: to crash together with violent impact.

gas pressure: the force of gas molecules hitting the surface of a container.

diameter: the line through the center of a circle, from one side to the other.

atmosphere: the blanket of air surrounding the earth.

exosphere: a very thin layer of gas surrounding a planet.

gravity: a force that pulls objects toward each other and all objects to the earth.

Each gas molecule travels at a different speed, but they all travel very fast. Temperature determines the average speed of molecules—the hotter they get, the faster the molecules travel. Even though gas molecules are very far apart relative to their size, they **collide** with each other a lot because they move so very fast.

Those collisions are what cause **gas pressure**. Gas pressure is the force of all the molecules colliding with the sides of a container. When fewer molecules are bouncing around and hitting the sides, the pressure is lower. More molecules hitting the sides of the container increases the pressure.

People use different types of GAS for many different things. In fact, without a very special gas, we wouldn't be here.

GAS IS GOOD FOR . . .

Oxygen is a gas found in the air we breathe. Your body needs oxygen to make energy so you can walk and run and even think. Sometimes, a person's body isn't able to absorb enough oxygen from the air, either because of illness or age. In this case, they might need an oxygen tank that delivers extra oxygen for breathing.

Another example of a useful gas is natural gas, which is made of mostly methane along with smaller amounts of carbon dioxide, nitrogen, or hydrogen sulfide. Natural gas comes from underground. We burn natural gas to heat our homes and cook on stoves.

Helium is a gas that's less dense than most gases, so it floats in normal air. You've probably seen floating balloons filled with helium. Helium is so much lighter than air that a 12-foot **diameter** balloon can lift someone weighing 57 pounds! Gases are a very important part of the world we live in.

The World's Ceiling

If gases expand to fill any container, why doesn't all the air just leave the earth? Actually, a bit of it does. In the top layer of the **atmosphere**, called the **exosphere**, some molecules do exit into space. Not very many, though, because the exosphere doesn't have many molecules compared with lower atmospheric layers, and many of those molecules don't have enough energy to escape the pull of **gravity**. The molecules that do escape are replaced by gases produced by volcanoes. Most air is held closer to Earth because of gravity's pull. The atmosphere slowly gets thinner (meaning fewer molecules) farther from Earth's surface until, at about 600 miles high, it merges into space.

The atmosphere is composed of these elements and compounds in a gaseous state:

> Nitrogen   78.1 percent

> Oxygen   20.9 percent

> Argon   0.93 percent

> Carbon dioxide   0.04 percent

> Neon   0.002 percent

> Helium   0.0005 percent

There are also trace amounts of methane, krypton, hydrogen, and water vapor. Even though water vapor is present only in amounts of 1 to 4 percent close to Earth, it is responsible for all our rain and weather.

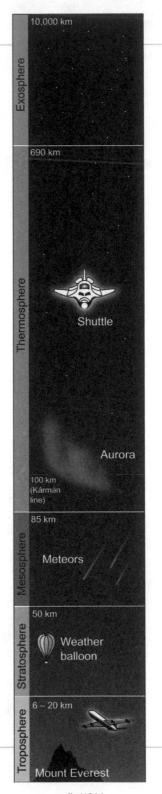

credit: NOAA

WORDS TO KNOW

Boyle's law: a gas law that states that, when temperature is held constant, as pressure increases, volume decreases. As pressure decreases, volume increases.

repel: to push away or apart.

compress: to press or squeeze something so that it fits into a smaller space.

calculus: a branch of mathematics that deals with calculating things such as the slopes of curves.

theory: an idea that tries to explain why something is the way it is.

BOYLE'S LAW

Robert Boyle (1627–1691) discovered one of the fundamental laws about gases. This law, now called **Boyle's law**, states that when pressure increases on a gas, the volume decreases—as long as the temperature stays the same. If you close the opening of a bicycle pump and press down on the handle, the volume decreases but the pressure increases and it gets harder and harder to push. Boyle had discovered the law, but he didn't know why gases acted this way and no one else did either.

Robert Boyle's notes on his air pressure experiments
credit: Wellcome Collection (CC BY 4.0)

Sir Isaac Newton developed a theory to explain this. He proposed that the particles, or molecules, of air are motionless and are held apart by forces that **repel** each other. Pushing on a gas, or applying pressure, is like pushing on a spring—it gets harder and harder as the spring **compresses**.

Because **GASES** have so much space between the **MOLECULES**, gases can be compressed, or squeezed, into a smaller space.

Now, Newton is possibly the greatest scientist who has ever lived. He developed **calculus** and described the fundamental laws of motion and gravity, among many other discoveries. Pretty smart guy! But, this time, he was wrong.

Newton's theory explained the facts beautifully. That's important to remember, because sometimes, a theory seems to fit the facts perfectly, but you may not have all the facts. That was the case for Newton—no one had all the facts yet, so his **theory** was wrong.

Later experiments showed that all molecules are always moving. Remember, even molecules in solids move by vibrating. Experiments also showed that molecules are attracted to each other. What does all this mean?

WORDS TO KNOW

equator: an invisible circle around the earth midway between the North and South Poles.

elevation: the height of something above sea level. Also called altitude.

atmospheric pressure: the amount of force pressing down on you by the weight of the air.

vacuum: a space that is empty of matter.

abhor: to hate.

The reason the pressure increases when a gas is compressed inside a container is because the molecules are always crashing into the sides of the container. When a molecule hits the sides, it exerts a force on the container, and it is the force of these crashes that causes gas pressure. When a container gets smaller, the molecules have less surface area to crash into, which raises the pressure.

Being wrong sometimes is necessary to achieve greatness—it means you're willing to take risks, which is an important part of being a scientist!

Water Bears!

Tardigrades, which are also called water bears or mossy piglets, are segmented animals smaller than the head of a pin. They look like a cute little gummi bear. But tardigrades are tough creatures. They can survive decades without water.

Some species of tardigrades can survive in extremely high or low pressures—as high as 6,000 times greater than our atmosphere or as low as outer space. They can be found living on top of Mount Everest, at the bottom of the ocean, in the Arctic, at the **equator**, in hot springs, and probably on some moss or lichen in your own backyard.

Take a close-up look at these remarkable creatures.

🔍 WaPo tardigrade

Popping Ears

Have your ears ever "popped" when going up or down quickly in an elevator or airplane? The atmosphere is always pressing on every part of us, and the lower the **elevation**, the greater the **atmospheric pressure**. We don't usually notice it because air inside our body is pressing out with the same pressure. When you come down quickly, though, your eardrums feel more pressure at the lower elevation and they push inward. Your body tries to compensate by allowing some air into the inner ear to balance the pressure on both sides of the eardrum. You can help by yawning, chewing gum, or swallowing. You can also try to take a deep breath and then pinch your nose. Keeping your mouth closed, try to gently breathe out through your nose. This will force air into small tubes that connect the inner ear to the throat.

VACUUMS

Vroom! A vacuum cleaner in your house works because a pump creates lower gas pressure in the tube. The pressure from the atmosphere stays the same, and it pushes the air—and some dirt along with it—into the vacuum.

Scientists use the term **vacuum** to mean a space without atoms or particles in it. You may have heard the phrase, "Nature **abhors** a vacuum." It's true, and it means that gases fill whatever container they're in.

The **PERFECT VACUUM** doesn't exist. Some molecules are always around—even in outer space. Space comes closest to a vacuum, though, with just a few HYDROGEN ATOMS per cubic centimeter of space. Scientists usually use the term "partial vacuum" instead of "perfect vacuum."

KITCHEN CHEMISTRY

Imagine you have a container that has a partition in the middle. The left side has no molecules and the right side has lots of molecules. If you pull out the partition, the molecules that are on the edge of the right side will bounce in every direction. Some of those molecules will bounce toward the left side, and because there won't be any molecules to get in their way, they'll keep going until they hit the side of the container. More and more molecules on the right side will do so. Because molecules travel so fast, the vacuum will be filled instantly.

Most **DECAFFEINATED** coffee has its caffeine removed using **SUPERCRITICAL** carbon dioxide!

WHEN GAS IS SUPERCRITICAL

Gases are almost always less dense than liquids because the molecules are so far apart. Remember, density is the mass in a given volume, or space. As the pressure on a gas increases, it gets denser because the molecules are squeezed closer together. After a certain point, the molecules are so close together that the gas turns into a liquid.

However, at a very high temperature, called the **critical temperature** of a gas, the gas won't turn into liquid no matter how high the pressure. At that point it's called a **supercritical fluid**.

You won't find this happening in your fireplace, though. You simply can't produce enough heat or high-enough pressure. The cores of stars have supercritical fluids, and the planet Jupiter has some gaseous layers that are supercritical and denser than water.

Now that we've covered all the different stages of matter, we can find out more about how matter shifts from state to state. Hint: Not by crossing state lines in a car!

ESSENTIAL QUESTION

Why does gas expand to fill a container?

EGG IN A
BOTTLE

TOOLBOX

° eggs
° clear glass or heavy plastic bottle with a neck slightly smaller than an egg
° paper
° match

Sometimes, you can see the effects of a change in air pressure. Try it with a hard-boiled egg!

CAUTION: Make sure you have an adult helper for this activity.

❯ **With an adult helper, hard boil an egg and peel it.**

❯ **Find a clear glass or heavy plastic bottle with a neck slightly smaller than the egg.** Large juice or sports drink bottles often work well.

❯ **Scrunch up a piece of paper and drop it into the bottle.** Have the egg ready.

❯ **With your adult helper, light a match and drop it into the bottle.** Immediately place the egg on top of the bottle opening. What happens? Record your observations in your science journal.

Think About It

What do you think happens to the temperature of the air when the flame burns? Remember that hot air takes up more space than cold air. Where does it go? You may have noticed the egg jumping on top of the bottle. The egg acts as a one-way valve, letting the hot air out of the bottle.

What do you think happens to the temperature of the air after the flame goes out? When the air cools, it takes up less space. This makes a partial vacuum, and the pressure from the air outside the bottle pushes the egg into the bottle.

MAKE YOUR OWN
MENTOS EXPLOSION

TOOLBOX

° index card
° 2-liter bottle of diet soda
° Mentos candies
° science journal and pencil

Chemical reaction or display of physical force? Try this experiment with candy and soda and see what happens.

CAUTION: This experiment should be done outside, ideally in the middle of a field or big lawn. Ask an adult to help you.

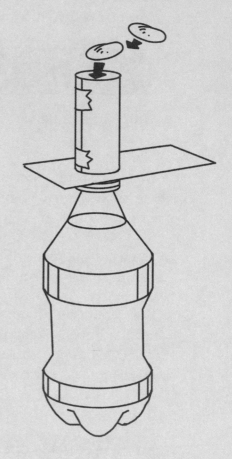

❯ **Roll an index card into a tube as wide as the opening of a 2-liter plastic soda bottle.** Tape the tube at the top and bottom.

❯ **Open a 2-liter diet soda bottle and set it on the ground away from people or objects.** Make sure it doesn't tip over.

❯ **Place your index-card tube on a second index card.** Then, open a roll of mint Mentos and stack seven Mentos in the tube. Place the tube and card on top of the opening of the bottle so that the tube is just over the opening, with the flat index card in between.

❯ **Being ready to move away, pull out the index card and let the Mentos slide into the soda.** Quickly stand back! What happens?

Try This!

Try some variations. Remember to vary only one thing at a time. Fruit Mentos are smoother than the mint kind—which makes a bigger explosion? What happens if you use regular soda instead of diet soda? How many Mentos produce the largest fountain? What if you crush the Mentos before putting them in the soda bottle? Do other candies work as well as Mentos? Record your observations in your science journal.

Chemical Reaction or Not?

Big chemical reaction, right? No! Most scientists believe that the soda whooshing out of the bottle is probably not a chemical reaction at all. Instead, physical forces are causing a lot of disruption. Here's how.

Soda is bubbly because it contains carbon dioxide—a gas—dissolved in water. That carbon dioxide was dissolved into the soda at the factory under high pressure. Remember, water molecules are strongly attracted to each other, and they surround the carbon dioxide, preventing lots of bubbles from forming. You can't see the carbon dioxide in a closed bottle, but when you open the bottle, you can see bubbles form and you can feel them fizzing in your mouth when you take a sip. The bubbles form because you have reduced the pressure, and the carbon dioxide comes out of the solution.

What happens when you shake a soda bottle first and then open it? Try it and see how it compares to the Mentos experiment—outside, of course. When you shake the bottle, the gas molecules can come together and form bubbles. Then, when you open the bottle, the carbon dioxide whooshes out of the bottle and takes some of the soda with it.

The Mentos have an effect similar to shaking a soda bottle—they allow gas bubbles to form. Remember, the carbon dioxide molecules are surrounded by water molecules that trap them. Once a bubble forms, it can grow very quickly. The trick is for the bubble to form in the first place. Rough surfaces allow more bubbles to form. These rough surfaces are places where a few carbon dioxide molecules can get together away from the water molecules. Once a few come together, others quickly follow. If you could look at a Mentos candy under a microscope, you would see that its surface is very uneven, with lots of nooks and crannies. These are the perfect places for bubbles—LOTS of bubbles—to form. When you drop the Mentos candies into the soda, they fall to the bottom, forming bubbles along the way. The bubbles form very quickly. They also rise to the surface very quickly, taking lots of soda with them.

SWIMMING **RAISINS**

See how gases can make things move!

❯ **Fill a tall, clear glass about two-thirds full of clear soda from a container you just opened.**

❯ **Put several raisins in the glass.** What happens? Draw what's happening in your science journal.

❯ **When the raisins are at the bottom of the glass,** do you see bubbles forming on them? The bubbles are carbon dioxide gas from the soda. Why do you think the raisins rise?

❯ **Look at the raisins that float to the top and then sink.** Do they have bubbles when they first sink? What do you think happened to the bubbles?

We breathe out carbon dioxide in **EVERY BREATH**—about one kilogram every day. Fortunately, plants absorb carbon dioxide, and use it with the energy from the sun **TO MAKE ENERGY.**

Try This!

Try this experiment with pieces of angel hair pasta instead of raisins. What's different? What's similar? Put in food coloring and use this as a fun centerpiece for a party.

Chapter 7

A CHANGE OF
STATE

If you hold a chocolate bar in your hand, after a few minutes you'll have a gooey (but delicious!) mess in your hands. What happened and why? And can you get your chocolate bar back?

As we've seen, all matter can exist in three different states: solid, liquid, and gas. When a substance changes from one of these states to another, it is called a change of state, or **phase change**. The most important thing to know about phase changes is that they aren't caused by a chemical reaction.

ESSENTIAL QUESTION

Why do substances change their state?

WORDS TO KNOW

phase change: the change from one state of matter—solid, liquid, or gas—to another.

83

WORDS TO KNOW

glacier: a slowly moving mass of ice and snow.

latent heat: the heat that is released or absorbed when a substance changes its state.

When a chocolate bar melts, the bonds within the molecules are not breaking apart and rearranging their atoms into new molecules, as would happen in a chemical reaction. Instead, the change from solid to liquid happens when enough heat is absorbed—in this case, heat from your hand—to break apart the strong bonds between the molecules so the molecules can slide over each other. The molecules themselves don't change, so no new substances are formed.

If you take that melted chocolate bar and place it in the refrigerator, it will become a solid (though not the original shape) candy bar again.

To understand why a substance CHANGES ITS STATE, first we must take a look at HEAT.

TEMPERATURE AND HEAT

Temperature and heat aren't the same thing. Temperature is a measure of the average speed at which particles are moving, and it's measured with a thermometer. Remember, the particles in all substances are in constant motion. In solids, the particles vibrate. In liquids, they slide over one another, and in gases, the particles bounce around at high speed.

At higher temperatures, the particles are vibrating or moving faster, on average. Heat is the total energy of all the particles in a substance. That means a **glacier** has more heat in it than a bowl of hot soup, simply because it's much bigger and has many more particles. It has a lower temperature, though, because on average, the molecules are moving much more slowly.

HEAT always flows from hot objects to cold objects.

This difference between heat and temperature is important when we talk about phase changes. When a solid turns into a liquid or a liquid becomes a gas, heat is absorbed to make the change. The heat, or energy, is used to break the bonds between the molecules. However, the molecules don't move any faster at first, so the temperature doesn't rise during the phase change. This heat is called **latent heat**, which is hidden heat.

Sweating is your body's way of removing heat.

KITCHEN CHEMISTRY

WORDS TO KNOW

sublimation: the change of a solid directly to a gas without passing through the liquid phase.

What happens if you add heat to water in its solid form, also called ice? Remember, all molecules are constantly moving, and even in solids such as ice, the molecules still vibrate. If you add heat to ice, its temperature will rise, making the molecules vibrate faster and faster. When the molecules are vibrating fast enough and the ice reaches 32 degrees Fahrenheit (0 degrees Celsius), there's enough energy to make the bonds between the molecules break. The ice changes to water!

As the ice is changing to water, all the heat goes into breaking those bonds. That means the temperature doesn't rise while the change is happening. All that energy goes toward changing the state of matter.

DEWDROPS form overnight when the air loses heat and the water that was present as a GAS cools enough to change into the LIQUID FORM. Dew! What happens to that dew as the air warms up from the sun?

Swamp Cooler

In very dry climates, people have used latent heat to help cool buildings. Windcatchers, which are devices that draw hot air across water to cool the air down, have been used for centuries in Persia, now called Iran. In fact, this method is still used there. Evaporative coolers, sometimes called swamp coolers, are used today in hot, dry areas such as the Desert Southwest of the United States. They pull hot, dry air across filters soaked with water. As the dry air passes through the filters, the water evaporates into the dry air. Because of latent heat, evaporation draws heat out of the air, cooling it down. Swamp coolers don't work in humid climates, however, because very little of the water evaporates. The next time you're sweltering hot, try hanging a damp sheet in front of a fan—making sure there's enough space between the two so the sheet doesn't catch on the fan blades. You can also try wrapping yourself in the sheet. If anyone asks what you're doing, say that you're harnessing the latent heat of evaporation.

When all the ice has changed to water, the temperature begins to rise again. This means the water molecules move faster and faster, forming clusters that move past each other. When the molecules are moving fast enough and the liquid reaches 212 degrees Fahrenheit (100 degrees Celsius), those molecule clusters break apart. The water changes to steam, or water vapor.

Just as with the solid-to-liquid change, during the liquid-to-gas change, the temperature doesn't rise. All of the heat goes into breaking the bonds. Once all the water has changed into steam, the temperature begins to rise as the gaseous molecules move faster and faster. In the reverse, when a gas turns into a liquid or a liquid into a solid, latent heat is released.

What states of matter are in this photo?

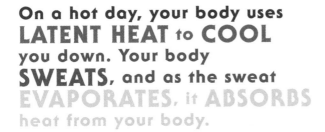

On a hot day, your body uses LATENT HEAT to COOL you down. Your body SWEATS, and as the sweat EVAPORATES, it ABSORBS heat from your body.

Sometimes, a solid turns directly into a gas, without going through the liquid state. This is called **sublimation,** and you can see its effects as close as your nearest freezer. Leave a full ice cube tray in your freezer for a very long time and you'll notice the ice cubes will shrink and eventually disappear. This is because the ice is sublimating, or going directly to a gas.

You may have seen sublimation on Halloween. Dry ice, which is frozen carbon dioxide, sublimates to a gas, forming a spooky-looking fog. That's because at room temperature and normal pressure, carbon dioxide is normally a gas, so it just changes directly from solid to gas.

WORDS TO KNOW

boiling point: the temperature at which a liquid boils, or turns to a gas. Different substances have different boiling points.

condensation: the process of a gas cooling down and changing into a liquid.

MELTING POINTS AND BOILING POINTS

Every substance has a melting point, the temperature at which the solid changes to a liquid. The opposite is the freezing point, the temperature at which a liquid changes to a solid. Melting and freezing are really the same process, just in opposite directions! Every substance also has a **boiling point**, the temperature at which a liquid changes to a gas. The opposite of the boiling point is the **condensation** point, when a gas changes to a liquid.

Solid water, or ice, melts to liquid water at about 32 degrees Fahrenheit (0 degrees Celsius). Gold melts at 1,947 degrees Fahrenheit (1,064 degrees Celsius) and tungsten (the element with the highest melting point) melts at about 6,192 degrees Fahrenheit (3,422 degrees Celsius).

Why do substances melt/freeze and boil/condense at different temperatures? The answer has to do with how strong the force of attraction between molecules is.

TUNGSTEN is used in nearly all incandescent light bulbs because of its extremely high melting point. A metal must be heated to very HIGH TEMPERATURES before it will emit light, and most metals melt before they reach that point!

A Fourth State of Matter

Some other states of matter exist, although we don't normally encounter them. The best known is plasma. In the plasma state, the electrons have been stripped from the atoms, leaving free electrons and bare nuclei. A plasma can be formed either by heating a gas to a very high temperature or by passing an electric current through a gas. The sun forms plasma naturally. In fact, plasma is actually the most common state of matter in the universe!

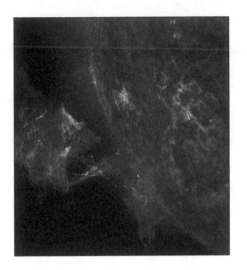

In a solid, the particles are tightly bound because there isn't enough energy from motion to overcome the strong bond of attraction. In a liquid, the particles are in clusters that come together and then move apart because the attraction and energy from motion are about equal in strength. In a gas, the particles bounce around quickly without being bound to each other. This is because the energy from the motion is much greater than the force of attraction pulling them together.

Remember, all PARTICLES are in constant MOTION, even those within a SOLID.

Substances have different melting and boiling points because they differ in how strongly their particles are attracted to each other. Tungsten, for example, has a very high melting point because the force of attraction between its atoms is very, very strong. It takes a lot of energy from motion, or a high temperature, to overcome the attraction force and break the bonds so that tungsten melts.

Ice, on the other hand, melts to water at a much lower melting point, because the force of attraction between its molecules is not as strong. It takes less energy from motion, or a lower temperature, to overcome the attractive force between the water molecules.

PROVING THE IMPOSSIBLE

If you put two containers in a freezer, one filled with hot water and one filled with cold water, which freezes first? The cold one, of course, because water must be very cold to freeze, right? In 1963, almost any chemistry or physics teacher would have thought it impossible for the hot container to freeze first.

Dr. Osborne told Erasto, **"THE FACTS,** as they are given, surprise me because they appear to **CONTRADICT** the **PHYSICS** I know."

In 1963, Erasto Mpemba was a schoolboy in Tanzania, a country in Africa. He and his friends loved to make ice cream at their school. They would boil milk, add sugar, let the mixture cool, and then put it in a freezer. The freezer never had enough room for all the ice cream, so the boys worked quickly to get space in the freezer.

One day, Erasto saw the freezer was filling up fast, so he put his ice cream in without cooling it first. When he came back later, his ice cream was ready, but that of another boy, who had put in a cooler ice cream mixture at the same time, was still a thick liquid. Erasto asked his science teacher how this could be, and they replied, "You were confused, that cannot happen."

A few years later, Erasto was studying heat in his high school physics class. Erasto asked the teacher how his hot ice cream mixture could have frozen before the cooler mixture. The teacher stated that Erasto must be confused.

Erasto insisted that he was not confused, and the teacher said, "Well, all I can say is that that is MPEMBA'S PHYSICS and not the UNIVERSAL PHYSICS."

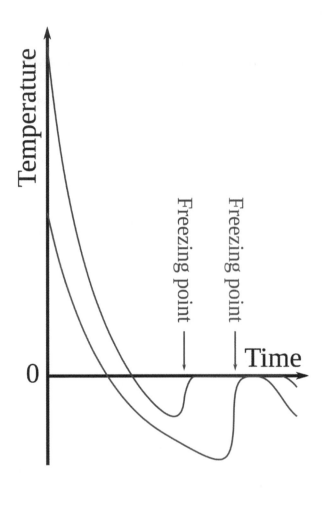

A graph showing the Mpemba effect
credit: Glglgl (CC BY 3.0)

From then on, whenever Erasto made a mistake, his classmates would say, "That is Mpemba's physics." But Erasto began to experiment with freezing hot and cold water.

KITCHEN CHEMISTRY

phenomenon: an observable fact or event.

supercooling: a liquid cooling below its freezing point without turning into a solid.

Mpemba effect: the name for a process where hot water can freeze faster than cold water.

Later, a university professor named Dr. Denis Osborne (1932–2014) visited the school, and Erasto told him of his experiments and again asked his question of how hot water can freeze faster than cold water. The professor thought Erasto was mistaken, but he wanted to encourage the students to question things. Erasto continued his experiments, demonstrating to his fellow students and teachers that hot water could indeed freeze faster than cold. Dr. Osborne got similar results.

Erasto Mpemba and Denis Osborne published a paper about this unusual **phenomenon** and proposed some explanations for it. Although scientists in earlier times had described this effect, modern science had forgotten it until the two rediscovered it.

Watch a video on the Mpemba effect. What practical applications of this can you think of?

 Mpemba effect video

Even today, no single explanation for this phenomenon is accepted by all scientists. One proposed reason is that as hot water cools, it evaporates. Evaporation takes away heat very quickly and also reduces the amount of water, which means less water to cool. Another reason could be that water can sometimes cool and stay liquid a few degrees below the temperature that water normally turns to ice at 32 degrees Fahrenheit (0 degrees Celsius) if it is not disturbed. This is called **supercooling**, and it happens more with water that starts cold than with water that starts hot.

Erasto Mpemba believed what he actually saw happen instead of what everyone expected to happen. Today, the unusual effect of very hot water freezing before cooler water is named for the young student who wouldn't take "impossible" for an answer: the **Mpemba effect**.

In your kitchen science lab, one substance is probably more abundant than anything else—water! In the next chapter, we'll dive deeper into this substance and find out what makes water so special.

ESSENTIAL QUESTION

Why do substances change their state?

THE MPEMBA
EFFECT

TOOLBOX
° 2 to 3 ceramic containers, the same size and shape
° water
° instant-read thermometer
° pot holders
° science journal

The Mpemba effect works under some conditions but not under others, and isn't completely understood. Do some experiments and see what you learn.

Caution: This project involves very hot water, so get an adult to help.

❱ **Select two or three containers that can hold very hot liquids.** Avoid metal containers—ceramics are a good choice. The containers must be the same size and shape because container shape can affect how fast a liquid cools.

❱ **Clear a space in the freezer that can fit all the containers.** If possible, make a big enough space so that the containers don't touch each other or the freezer walls.

❱ **With your adult helper, fill a saucepan with water and heat to almost boiling.** When the water is close to boiling, run the tap water until the water is as hot as you can get it, ideally between 140 and 150 degrees Fahrenheit (60 to 65 degrees Celsius).

❱ **Measure 1 cup (or whatever amount will mostly fill your container) of hot tap water into one container.** Quickly measure exactly the same amount of almost boiling water into the second container. If you have a third container, measure the same amount of cold tap water into it.

❱ **Using pot holders for the containers with hot liquid, immediately place all three containers in the freezer.** Remember to try to avoid having the containers touch each other or the freezer walls.

❱ **Check your containers every 10 minutes or so to see which container freezes first.** What do you notice? Record your observations in your science journal.

Try This!

Try the experiment again, changing one variable at a time to see what makes a difference. Variables could include the size and shape of the containers, whether the containers are heated first, and the location of the containers in the freezer.

VANILLA
ICE CREAM

One of the best things about kitchen chemistry is delicious "science experiments!"

❯ **Pour the milk, cream, sugar, and vanilla into one of the quart plastic bags and seal.** Try not to leave too much air in the bag. Place this bag into the other quart bag and seal.

❯ **Place one cup of ice into the large bag.** With a thermometer, take the temperature of the ice, then add ½ cup salt. Record the temperature in your science journal.

Ice Cream

Ice cream is made different ways and has different names in countries around the world. In Italy, it's called gelato. In India, kulfi. And in Japan, mochi.

Before there was ice cream, there was flavored ice. Long ago, King Solomon enjoyed iced drinks, and the Greeks, Romans, and Arabs drank flavored ice drinks. Before there were refrigerators, the problem was how to freeze food. People would bring ice from high in mountains, where it was colder, and then store the ice in caves or deep pits. The first time milk was used in a frozen treat was in China a little before 700 CE. They mixed milk and flour and flavoring, then put the mixture into metal tubes and lowered the tubes into an ice pool.

But it wasn't until the 1660s that Antonio Latini (1642–1692) made the first official ice cream in Italy. Still, it was expensive and only enjoyed by the upper class.

That started to change in 1843, when Nancy Johnson (1794–1880) invented a hand-crank ice cream maker and refrigerators began to be used.

Today, in the United States, 9 percent of all cow's milk is used to make ice cream, and 1.6 billion gallons of ice cream are produced each year!

> **Place the small bag in the large bag.** Fill the large bag with the rest of the ice, add the rest of the salt, and seal.

> **Cover the bag with a cloth to protect your hands from the cold.** Gently shake the large bag from side to side for about 15 minutes or until the ice cream is solid.

> **Open the large bag.** Take the temperature of the ice-salt-water mixture and record it in your science journal. Did the temperature change?

> **Wipe off the top of the small bag,** open carefully, and . . . yum! Add any toppings you like. If the ice cream is too soft for your liking, put it in the freezer for a few minutes to harden. Does the ice cream taste like you'd expect from the ingredients? Think about whether there was a chemical reaction. Is this the demonstration of a physical or a chemical change?

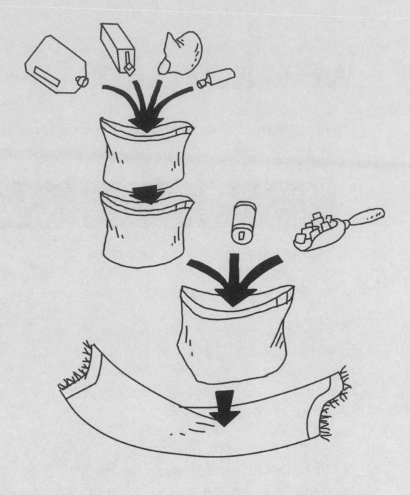

Try This!

Try this again, but don't add salt to the ice. What happens? Salt lowers the melting point of water below 32 degrees Fahrenheit (0 degrees Celsius), which means that water freezes and ice melts at a lower temperature. Salt dissolves in water, separating into sodium and chloride ions. These ions get in the way of the water molecules forming a crystal structure. The whole slushy ice-salt-water mixture is colder than the normal freezing point of water.

CRUSH A CAN
WITH NO HANDS

TOOLBOX
- bowl of ice water
- empty soda can
- saucepan
- oven mitts
- tongs

Try this experiment to see how just a little water can crush a soda can!

Caution: This project involves boiling water, and the can and liquid get VERY hot, so get an adult to help, especially when turning the can over into the ice.

❯ **Fill a bowl with ice water and place it next to the stove.** Pour enough tap water into an empty soda can to cover the bottom.

❯ **Place a saucepan on the stove and cover the bottom with about 2 inches of tap water.** Put on oven mitts, and heat the water in the saucepan until boiling. With your adult helper, use tongs to hold the can in the boiling water.

❯ **When steam comes out of the can opening, wait one minute, then use the tongs to carefully and quickly flip the can upside down into the bowl of ice water.** Be careful not to let the boiling water inside the can splash on you. What happens? Why?

WHAT'S HAPPENING?

When the water in the can is heated, it boils and turns into gaseous water, called water vapor. The water vapor pushes out some of the air in the can. When you turn the can upside down into the ice, the water vapor quickly cools down from losing heat to the icy water and surrounding air, and it turns back into liquid water. Liquid water takes up much less space than water vapor, but no air can get in to fill the space, so a partial vacuum forms inside the can. The outside air pressure stays the same. The difference between the outside and inside pressure is greater than the strength of the can, and it is crushed.

Chapter 8

WATER
EVERYWHERE

Water is all around us. It's in the paper used for this book. It's in the furniture we sit on. It's in the air. And it's in you. Almost everything you can see and touch has at least a tiny amount of water in it. In fact, Earth is sometimes called the "blue planet" because more than 71 percent of the planet is covered in water!

You might think that because water is everywhere, it's a very simple substance. Not true! Water has some very unusual properties. That's a good thing, because those unusual properties make it possible for us to skate on frozen ponds, for fish to survive the winter, for plants to grow, and even for there to be life at all.

ESSENTIAL QUESTION

Why is water special?

KITCHEN CHEMISTRY

WORDS TO KNOW

polarity: the quality of a molecule having one end with a negative charge and the other end with a positive charge.

surfactant: short for "surface active agent." A substance, such as soap, that lowers the surface tension of a liquid.

We've talked a lot about water in earlier chapters, so you may recall that the chemical formula for water is H_2O. This means that water is made up of two hydrogen atoms and one oxygen atom. Look at the diagram below—the oxygen atom has a minus sign on it and the hydrogen atoms have a plus sign. That's because the oxygen atom has a stronger pull on the electrons, which have a negative charge—this pulls them closer. That means the area around the oxygen atom is negative and the areas around the hydrogen atoms are positive.

When one end of a molecule has a slight negative charge and one end a positive charge, the molecule is polar. The **polarity** also gives water molecules a shape similar to a "V."

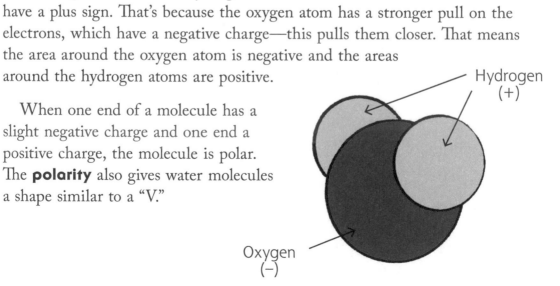

Hydrogen (+)

Oxygen (−)

Baby Lungs

Our lungs use small air sacs, like balloons, to breathe. These air sacs are coated with water and a natural **surfactant**. Water has a high surface tension, so these tiny air sacs would collapse when we breathe out if they didn't have surfactant—just like water bubbles collapse without dish soap. And every new breath would take a lot of force, like blowing up a new balloon. Premature babies do not have enough of this surfactant, and their lungs can't expand on their own. Understanding surface tension has allowed doctors to manufacture surfactants to help these babies breathe until they can make their own.

Since positive and negative charges are attracted to each other, the oxygen end of a water molecule is attracted to the hydrogen end of other water molecules. The oxygen end is also attracted to other positively charged particles—such as the sodium in salt. Because of this, water's polarity allows it to dissolve many substances that humans and animals need and transport those substances to different parts of the body.

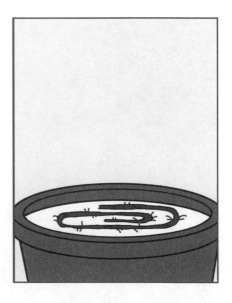

KITCHEN CHEMISTRY

WORDS TO KNOW

surface tension: the force that holds together molecules on the surface of a liquid so that the liquid acts like it has a stretchy skin. Water has a high surface tension.

malaria: a blood disease caused by parasites often found in jungle and rainforest environments. It is spread by mosquitoes.

SURFACE TENSION

Try putting a drop of water on wax paper or glass and look at it closely. Does it look like it has a skin? There really isn't a skin—what you're seeing is **surface tension**.

The molecules in water are attracted to each other, like tiny magnets, because the hydrogen atom in one molecule is attracted to the oxygen atom in another molecule. Every water molecule feels pulled toward the others, so the water molecules shrink away from the surface and cling to each other.

Take a look at the life of a water strider in this video.

🔎 water strider Deep Look

PS

Agnes Pockels

Agnes Pockels (1862–1935) was born in Germany in 1862. At that time, women in Germany could not go to college. Pockels loved science and excelled in school, so when women were later allowed to attend college, she wanted to go. But her parents became ill with **malaria** and she needed to be home to take care of them. Pockels stayed interested in science, however, reading any textbooks she could find and trying out her own experiments. While washing dishes, she studied the surface tension of water and noticed that different things affected the surface tension. Using bowls, string, and buttons, she made the first-ever device to measure surface tension. Because Pockels didn't have a college degree and was unknown in the world of science, she couldn't publish a paper about her findings, so she sent her information to Lord Rayleigh, the same scientist who followed up on Benjamin Franklin's experiments with oil and water. Lord Rayleigh was so impressed with her work that he sent it to *Nature* magazine, a famous science journal, which published the letter. She continued her research on surfaces and solutions for more than 40 years, publishing more papers on her own and winning awards. Some of her scientific methods are still used today. Agnes Pockels did all her work in the laboratory at her home—her kitchen!

Have you ever seen a water strider travel across the surface of water? It can do that because of surface tension! Water striders' legs have thousands of tiny hairs, each about two-thousandths of an inch long. The hairs have tiny grooves that trap air. All those tiny hairs are held up by the surface tension of the water. Try the projects at the end of the chapter to see just how strong surface tension can be or what happens when the surface tension of water is lowered.

SURFACE TENSION causes water to take the shape that has the smallest surface area, which is why a drop of water takes the shape of a sphere.

aquifer: an underground layer of rock that has space in it that holds water.

microorganism: a living thing that is so small you can see it only with a microscope.

EXPANDING WATER

When water freezes, it expands, or gets bigger. This may not seem like a big deal but it is. Nearly every other liquid shrinks when it becomes a solid. That's because a liquid has more energy than a solid, and the molecules usually need more room to move around.

Remember that water is polar, with a slightly negative end, and a slightly positive end. This allows it to form weaker bonds with other molecules. In liquid water, these weaker bonds form and break over and over. But when the temperature drops and water becomes a solid, the weaker bonds stay in place. The bonds form a rigid crystal structure—ice—that takes up more space than liquid water. That means ice is less dense that water.

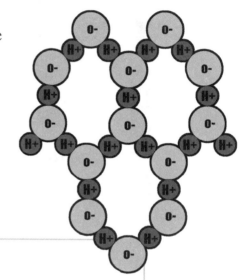

Where's the Water?

Your body is mostly water, although the amount decreases as you get older. When you were a baby, about 74 percent of your body was water. At age 10, about 60 percent of your body is water. When you're 70 years old, about 56 percent will be water if you're male and about 47 percent if you're female.

Water covers about 71 percent of the surface of Earth. Most of it is in the oceans and in ice at the North and South Poles, but water is also in clouds, rain, rivers, lakes, and underground **aquifers**. In outer space, frozen water has been found on the moon, on planets—particularly Mercury, Mars, Neptune, and Pluto—and in comets and clouds between stars in our galaxy. Recent explorations of Mars indicate that there might be liquid water underground on Mars. This means **microorganisms** could be living there!

Because ice is less dense than water, it floats on top of it. When pond water freezes, the ice floats on top and the water beneath is insulated from the colder air. People can skate on the ice on top, and fish can live underneath in cold, but not frozen, water. If ice were heavier than water, it would sink to the bottom and the water above would not be insulated. The entire pond would freeze. The fish and other aquatic creatures wouldn't be able to survive.

Your brain is made of **73 PERCENT WATER,** and your lungs are **83 PERCENT WATER.** But that's nothing compared to a jellyfish or cucumber—they're made of **95% WATER!**

See how water molecules change as liquid water reaches its freezing point.

🔎 NBC News chemistry of ice

EIFFEL PLASTERER
(1899–1989), a high school science teacher who experimented with bubbles, blew a bubble that lasted for 341 days!
SIR JAMES DEWAR
(1842–1923), a Scottish chemist and physicist, made a disc of soap film that lasted **more than three years!**

WHAT'S IN A BUBBLE?

If you turn on the water full blast in the kitchen sink and look closely, you'll see bubbles form and disappear very quickly. That's because the surface tension pulls on the bubbles and makes them collapse.

If you add dish soap to water, it lowers the surface tension and bubbles last much longer. But what is a bubble really? It's two layers of soap molecules, also called surfactant, surrounding a layer of water molecules. The film of a soap bubble is about the thinnest thing that you can see with just your eyes. It's about 5,000 times thinner than a human hair! Soap films always take up the smallest area possible, which means a bubble is always a sphere.

Frei Otto (1925–2015), an architect and engineer, used soap bubbles and films as models for the tent-like buildings he designed, because soap films always use the least area. These are very efficient shapes! Otto designed the roof for the 1972 Olympic Stadium in Munich, Germany.

1972 Munich Olympic stadium designed by Frei Otto
credit: Timothy Brown (CC BY 2.0)

Look back over your science journal and think about the experiments you've tried. What did you learn about the way substances behave? What might be causing things to happen in the world around you?

Remember, not everything happens the way you think it did, so be open to new explanations. Even Sir Isaac Newton, one of the smartest scientists ever, sometimes got it wrong because he didn't have all of the information he needed. Whenever you try something, be sure it's safe and try to predict what will happen. Sometimes, when things don't happen like you predict, you can learn even more trying to figure out what happened.

When you look at all of the incredible variety of things around us, it's remarkable that everything is made from 94 different kinds of atoms. The way those atoms bond together and the way they're arranged—like being solid, liquid, gas, or plasma—determine how everything around you looks, smells, sounds, tastes, and feels. It's an amazing universe we live in, and it's all shaped by chemistry.

We have the same amount of water on Earth now as there was more than 4 BILLION YEARS AGO—it just gets recycled. The water you drink might have molecules THAT A DINOSAUR DRANK!

ESSENTIAL QUESTION

Why is water special?

ICE
SPIKES

TOOLBOX
° ice cube tray
° rainwater or distilled water
° science journal and pencil

What happens as an ice cube freezes? Find out in this experiment.

❯ **Fill a plastic ice cube tray with rainwater or distilled water from the grocery store.** Place it in the freezer in a way that you can observe the top of the tray without disturbing it.

❯ **Every 30 minutes, observe the tray and record in your science journal how the ice is forming.** You can describe it or draw a picture. Do you expect the ice to form at the top of the cubes first or the bottom? Think about which is denser, ice or water. Do you think it will form in the middle first or from the sides?

❯ **After a few hours, check your ice cubes again.** You should see spikes of ice on some of the cubes. The time it takes to see them depends on your freezer. If you don't see spikes, then try again, making sure to use distilled water. This experiment works best in a regular frost-free freezer, not a deep (sub-zero) freezer.

WHAT'S HAPPENING?

Ice will form on the edges first at the surface, and work its way inward until only a small hole is left in the middle. Ice takes up more space than water (which is why it's less dense), so as more ice forms underneath, the water that's left has nowhere to go and it's forced up through the hole. Bit by bit, more water is pushed up through the hole, and it freezes into a spike.

Try This!

Try using containers of different sizes and shapes. If you live in an area where it snows in winter, try this experiment outside at different temperatures to see what happens. Do more or fewer spikes form as the temperature drops? Why do you think that might be?

WATER THAT
BENDS

Surface tension might seem like magic, but it's all science. Do some experiments to see how it works.

❯ **Hold a paper clip or needle vertically and drop it into a bowl of water.** Why do you think it sinks?

❯ **Take the paper clip out.** Place it on a fork and hold it parallel to the water. Slowly lower the fork into the water. The paper clip should stay on top of the water.

❯ **Look closely at the water around the paper clip.** Do you see the water bend as it touches the paper clip? You probably never thought that water could bend!

WHAT'S HAPPENING?

The paper clip is not actually floating. If it could float, it would do so no matter how you put it in the water. But when you slowly lower the paper clip, it lightly rests on the "skin" of the water, held up by the force of the surface tension. The surface tension has enough force to counteract the force of gravity that pulls on the paper clip.

Try This!

Which force—surface tension or gravity—would win out if you put a marble on top of the water? Try different objects. Do they sink or float or does surface tension hold them up?

Add a drop of dish soap to the surface of the water near the paper clip. Now what happens? Remember what soap does to surface tension.

MARBLEIZED
PAPER

Science and art go together like cookies and milk! See what you can create in this project.

❱ **Spread out several sheets of newspaper and place a large, shallow pan on top.** Spread extra newspaper as a drying area. Pour a thin layer of whole milk in the pan, enough to cover the entire bottom of the pan.

❱ **Add a few drops of food coloring to the center of the pan.** Add a few drops of a second color next to the first color. Add a drop or two of liquid dish soap in between the two colors. You can also dip a cotton swab in the dish soap and then touch the tip to the center of the pan and hold it there for 10 seconds.

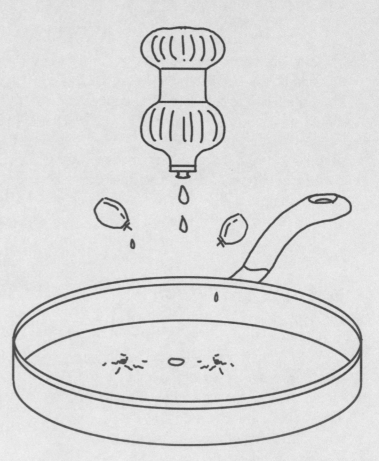

❱ **If you like, gently and slowly drag a stick or fork through the colors.** See if you can get thin tendrils of color to swirl around.

❱ **Place a sheet of watercolor paper flat onto the surface design and quickly take it off again.** Lay the paper, color side up, on the newspaper to dry. Swirl the colors around some more until they become gray, then dump the milk and food color mixture into the sink.

Easy Ways to Conserve Water!

Don't let the water run while rinsing dishes, and soak pots and pans instead of letting the water run while you scrape them clean.

Adjust sprinklers so only your lawn is watered and not the house, sidewalk, or street.

Use the garbage disposal sparingly. Compost vegetable food waste instead and save gallons every time.

For cold drinks, keep a pitcher of water in the refrigerator instead of running the tap. This way, every drop goes down you and not the drain.

If your shower fills a one-gallon bucket in less than 20 seconds, replace the showerhead with a water-efficient model.

Shorten your shower by a minute or two and you'll save up to 150 gallons per month.

WHAT'S HAPPENING?

Milk is mostly water, but it also has fat molecules, which are nonpolar and don't dissolve in water, which is polar. The soap molecules have one end that is polar and one end that is nonpolar, so the soap comes between the water and fat. The soap molecules zip around, trying to bond with the fat, and the food coloring gets carried along for the ride, making a beautiful swirl of color!

Try This!

Try this with other liquids instead of whole milk, such as water, cream, or skim milk, and predict which you think will work best. (Hint: Which liquid has the most fat molecules?) Record the differences in your science journal. Try dripping the different food colors on top of each other or just around the outside. Try dipping the cotton swab with dishwashing liquid in different places.

MAKE SOME
BUBBLES!

Try making your own bubble solution, then try some of the following different ways of making bubbles. If you're working indoors, put down newspaper first. If you're outside, try this when there's no wind. Humid days work well. Feel free to use your hands in the bubble solution, but if your hands are dry, they'll pop the bubbles, so wet them before touching bubbles.

❱ **Pour about a half gallon of water into a pie pan, baking dish, or large tray.** If possible, use distilled water. Gently but thoroughly mix about a half cup dishwashing soap into the water. You can double the recipe if you want the bubble solution to be deeper.

❱ **Skim off any foam from the top. Add 1 tablespoon glycerin or corn syrup.** After letting the bubble solution sit for a day, make some bubbles. Hold your hands so your thumbs and index fingers form a hoop shape. Dip your hands in the bubble solution and pull them out. Gently blow, and when you have a bubble you like, push your hands together to close off the hoop shape and release the bubble.

Bubbles in Space!

Bubbles in space behave differently from bubbles on Earth! Bubbles take the round shape we are familiar with because of air pressure acting on the outside and inside of the sphere. But in space, there's no air pressure. Any bubble you try to blow would burst almost instantly. In a spaceship, however, you can blow bubbles, though they work a little differently. There is air pressure, but no gravity. This means a regular soap bubble might last longer in a spaceship than on Earth, since there is no gravity to pull the heavier liquids to the bottom of the bubble. Water behaves differently, too. Because of that lack of gravity, air bubbles in the water linger instead of rising to the surface. In fact, water with lots of air bubbles looks more like a gel than water!

TAKE IT FURTHER

Try some of these variations on bubbles.

❭ **Get two plastic drinking straws.** Cut some cotton string about six times as long as one straw. Pull the string through each of the straws so that you have a rectangle, with the straws forming two sides opposite each other, and string forming the other two sides. Knot the ends of the string together to form a loop.

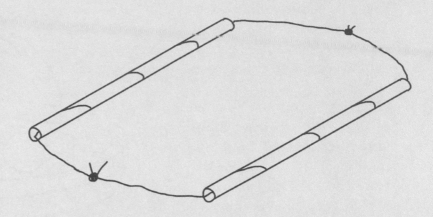

❭ **Hold one straw in each hand and dip the rectangle into the bubble solution.** Lift up and slowly pull the straws apart. You should have a soap film.

❭ **Hold the frame in front of you, just below your waist.** Pull the frame up and slightly towards you and walk slowly backwards. To release the bubble, pull the frame up as you bring the straws together. You can also try twisting the straws in opposite directions. Practice over and over!

Try making different kinds of bubbles.

❯ **Dip a straw into the bubble solution. Hold the straw just above the bubble solution and blow gently.** When you have a bubble almost as big as a tennis ball, pull the straw out. Poke the bubble with a dry pencil. What happens? Blow another bubble, get the pencil wet, and poke it.

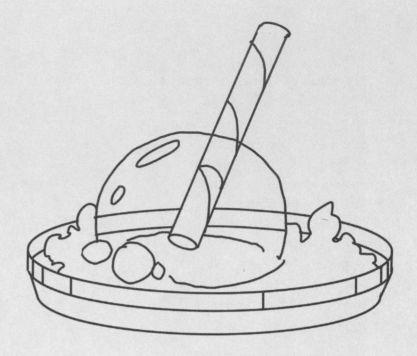

❯ **Carefully push the wet end of the straw into the bubble until it touches the bubble mix on the cookie sheet.** Slowly blow a bubble inside the first bubble. Can you blow more than one bubble inside the first one?

❯ **Try blowing very gently or very quickly into the bubble solution, exploring different kinds of bubbles.** Use different shapes to blow bubbles. You can form pipe cleaners into stars, letters, boxes, or any other shape, as long as the shape is closed.

Want a super-size bubble extravaganza? Try this outside on a calm, warm day.

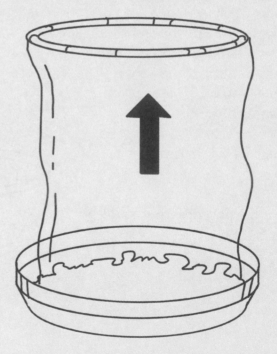

❯ **Wrap yarn or cloth around a Hula Hoop, like a candy cane.** Fill the bottom of a round kiddie swimming pool that's slightly larger than the Hula Hoop with bubble solution, about 3 inches deep. Set the Hula Hoop into the solution and get it completely wet. Have one person step inside the Hula Hoop and two others stand on either side outside the pool, and wet their hands. The two should pull the Hula Hoop up and above the first person's head. Try pulling at different speeds to see what works best. How tall can you make the bubble?